Toronto Sketches 10

MIKE FILEY

Toronto
Sketches

10

DUNDURN PRESS
TORONTO

Editor: Jennifer McKnight
Design: Courtney Horner
Printer: Webcom

Library and Archives Canada Cataloguing in Publication

Filey, Mike, 1941-
     Toronto sketches 10 : "the way we were" / by Mike Filey.

Issued also in an electronic format.
ISBN 978-1-55488-780-4

     1. Toronto (Ont.)-History. I. Title. II. Title: Toronto sketches ten.

FC3097.4.F5497 2010   971.3'541   C2010-902678-0

1   2   3   4   5   14   13   12   11   10

We acknowledge the support of the **Canada Council for the Arts** and the **Ontario Arts Council** for our publishing program. We also acknowledge the financial support of the Government of Canada through the **Canada Book Fund** and **Livres Canada Books**, and **Livres Canada Books**, and the **Government of Ontario** through the **Ontario Book Publishers Tax Credit program**, and the **Ontario Media Development Corporation**.

Care has been taken to trace the ownership of copyright material used in this book. The author and the publisher welcome any information enabling them to rectify any references or credits in subsequent editions.

J. Kirk Howard, President

Printed and bound in Canada.
www.dundurn.com

Unless otherwise credited, all photos are from the collection of Mike Filey.

Dundurn Press	Gazelle Book Services Limited	Dundurn Press
3 Church Street, Suite 500	White Cross Mills	2250 Military Road
Toronto, Ontario, Canada	High Town, Lancaster, England	Tonawanda, NY
M5E 1M2	LA1 4XS	U.S.A. 14150

Mixed Sources
Product group from well-managed forests, and other controlled sources
www.fsc.org Cert no. SW-COC-002358
© 1996 Forest Stewardship Council
FSC

For my wife Yarmila

Contents

Mike Filey's column "The Way We Were" has appeared in the *Toronto Sunday Sun* on a regular basis since 1975. Many of his earlier columns have been reproduced in volumes 1 through 9 of Dundurn Press's Toronto Sketches series. The columns in this book originally appeared in 2007, 2008, and 2009. Appended to each column is the date it first appeared as well as any relevant material that may have surfaced since that date (indicated by an asterisk).

A Watery Commute

Every once in a while I get stumped for a subject for my AM 740 morning feature. Then, like a gift out of the blue, a suggestion will be made that we do something that's never been done before. Take, for instance, the notion of connecting Etobicoke and Scarborough with downtown Toronto by ferry or the concept of a Toronto to Hamilton commuter boat, a sort of a GO Boat as Transportation Minister Donna Cansfield called it. New ideas? Hardly.

Though not exactly a Lake Ontario commuter service such as the TTC is intending to investigate, Torontonians were able to travel to and from the mouth of the Humber River in old Etobicoke Township as far back as the 1870s. Usually the trips were for pleasure, with one of the main destination points being John Duck's Wimbleton House hotel on the west bank where the river emptied into the lake. Here he constructed a dock to accommodate the various steamboats that frequently arrived from the big city, often filled to capacity with pleasure seekers. To make an outing to the Wimbleton House even more exciting, John Duck opened a zoo that came complete with bears, raccoons, deer, mink, and a collection of other animals that inhabited the Etobicoke hinterland.

Duck's place wasn't the only destination for the Toronto-based steamers. Long Branch, Oakville, and Bronte also drew big crowds, while Lorne Park was especially popular with its Hotel Louise, amusement park, tennis courts, and picnic grounds. When the province built the Toronto-Hamilton highway

Artist Clarence Duff sketched this charming view depicting the steamboat wharf at Lorne Park in 1898.

during the first war the (we now call it Highway 2), the steamboats gave way to quicker and more reliable travel by automobile and the roads have been plugged ever since.

While these examples of water-borne traffic were popular, primarily during the warm summer months, there was a period of time starting in 1886 when there was, in fact, a regular passenger service in place between Toronto and Hamilton. That service was provided by several small ocean-going vessels, two of which were called the *Macassa* and the *Modjeska*. Operated by the Hamilton Steamship Company, each carried seven hundred to eight hundred passengers and had a top speed of twenty-three miles per hour. Contemporary accounts describe the trip as being as regular and speedy as a similar trip by train. The only drawback, however, was the passenger and ticketing facilities at the Toronto end of the voyage that were described as being somewhat chaotic due to the capital city's unsettled waterfront question. Even back then they weren't sure what was going on along Toronto's waterfront.

Turbinia was the fastest passenger boat on the Great Lakes. The turbine-powered vessel provided a daily commuter service between Toronto and Hamilton for many years early in the twentieth century.

Increasing passenger traffic between the two cities eventually resulted in the formation of a new company, the Hamilton Turbine Steamship Company, and the introduction of a remarkable new passenger vessel, the *Turbinia*. As both the company's and vessel's name suggest, this new craft was powered not by reciprocal steam engines, as were used on the other passenger boats, but by three coal-fired steam turbine engines, giving the Newcastle-on-Tyne-built vessel a top speed of thirty miles per hour. It was said that *Turbinia* could easily outdistance any other steamer on Lake Ontario.

For a number of years, commuters had a choice of three craft on board which to make the Toronto–Hamilton trip, some of them doing the trip four times each weekday. The competition lasted until 1913 when all three vessels came under the control of the newly organized Canada Steamship Lines Ltd. *Turbinia* was requisitioned soon after the Great War broke out and for a number of years she saw service as a troop transport between England and France.

Returning to the Toronto-Hamilton service in 1923, *Turbinia* was now one of two on that run, *Modjeska* having been sold to an Owen Sound company. In 1927 *Turbinia* was re-assigned to the Montreal–Quebec City run. That lasted but a short time and in 1937 she was unceremoniously scrapped. The Toronto-Hamilton passenger boat service ended when the *Macassa* was withdrawn and, like her one-time running mate *Modjeska*, sent to Owen Sound.

Will passenger boat service between these two large communities ever return? Will there be GO boats? Stranger things have happened.

July 15, 2007

Cronyism Has Always Existed Here

The old photograph is from the City of Toronto Archives and was snapped on July 11, 1950. It looks north on Yonge Street over Dundas and was taken to document conditions prior to the TTC beginning preliminary work on the construction of this section of the new Yonge subway. Note the Peter Witt streetcar to extreme right of the view. Operating on the Yonge route it has diverted from lower Yonge Street (via Richmond, Victoria, and Dundas Streets) owing to subway construction in and around the Yonge and Queen intersection. At the northeast corner of the view is the Brown Derby Tavern that opened on this corner in December 1949. The Derby's first ads identified it as the

"Gayest Spot in Town," a description with a much different meaning back then. Performers appearing at the Tavern's "Tin Pan Alley" room were Gene Rogers, the Tune-Toppers, and Paula Watson. Further up Yonge Street is the Biltmore Theatre, Le Coq d'Or, The Friars, Steeles Tavern, The Edison Hotel, and of course, A&A Records and Sam the Record Man.

The second photo shows a similar view. Just out of the view to the right is Yonge-Dundas Square that was officially opened in 2003. At the northeast corner of the intersection, and still under construction, is the newly named Toronto Life Square (formerly Metropolis), that when completed will feature a mix of offices, shops, and restaurants, as well as a multi-screen theatre complex. The exterior of the structure will feature a thirty foot by fifty-two foot high-definition video display screen, the nation's largest.

The two portraits depict the gentlemen for whom this intersection and, more recently, the nearby Square were named. To understand why the names of Sir George Yonge and Sir Henry Dundas were selected one must realize that John Graves Simcoe, our province's first lieutenant governor, was eager to make sure that those people back in England who could influence his successes in the new world were recognized. What better way to do so than to name major thoroughfares in their honour? Sir George was a good friend and a member of the cabinet of King George III, the reigning British monarch when our city was established by John Graves Simcoe. Sir George was also an expert on the subject of Roman road building. A perfect person, in Simcoe's mind at least, to honour in the name of this newly constructed military road.

Sir Henry Dundas was also a personal friend who served in various influential positions in the British government. Another obvious choice.

Today, many would criticize such obvious cronyism. However, to make sure his new responsibilities, the Province of Upper Canada (renamed Ontario in 1867), and a fledgling community he called York (the name was changed to Toronto in 1834) would succeed, Simcoe did whatever he could to get the help he would surely need. Street naming was one easy way to do just that.

October 28, 2007

Toronto Under Siege

When it comes to important dates in the early years of our community's history, several immediately come to mind: September 19, 1615, Étienne Brûlé becomes first European to see the future site of Toronto; May 2, 1793, John Graves Simcoe, the province's first lieutenant governor, visits an area on the north shore of Lake Ontario that he has selected as the site of his "royal" Town of York; August 1, 1805, a revised version of the still controversial "Toronto Purchase" agreement between the Mississauga Nation and The Crown is signed; March 6, 1834, Simcoe's Town of York is elevated to the status of city and its name changed to Toronto; July 1, 1867, Toronto becomes the capital of the new Province of Ontario.

And then there's April 27, 1813. That was the day that American military forces laid siege to our community. The attack was part of what has become known as the War of 1812, although a more accurate term would have been "James Madison's War" since it was the American president who was particularly eager to take revenge on the British government for its interference in his young nation's affairs. One way to take out that revenge was to attack Britain's colonies in Upper and Lower Canada (now Ontario and Quebec, respectively). In fact, Madison predicted that when his forces crossed the border Canadians would welcome them with open arms. Before long we'd all be one happy family basking under the Stars and Stripes.

Courtesy of the National Archives of Canada.

York Barracks, the name by which our present Fort York was originally known, as sketched by Lt. Sempronius Stretton in 1804. It had changed little when American forces attacked both it and the town just nine years later.

But the president was wrong, and though numerous deadly battles took place during the thirty or so months that hostilities took place all along the U.S.-Canada border the belief that Britain would lose her grip on the colonies never came to pass.

One of the most serious conflicts took place exactly 195 years ago today when enemy forces on board a flotilla of U.S. naval vessels overwhelmed the seven hundred inhabitants of our community, then (and until 1834) called York. The fighting was fierce with many on both sides falling victim to cannon and rifle fire, and hundreds more eventually succumbing to wounds and sickness.

Over the following days the occupying forces burned several buildings, looted private dwellings, and destroyed quantities of public records before sailing away, leaving the citizens of York dejected, but unbroken.

While the rest of the story is far too lengthy to record in this column, there is a marvellous book that is the most comprehensive yet published. With well-researched text, numerous photos, sketches, and maps, and all-inclusive appendices, this hardcover volume describes in great detail not just the attack on our community and the sad aftermath, but numerous other aspects of the War of 1812 as well. *Capital in Flames, the American Attack on York, 1813* by Robert Malcomson is from the Robin Brass Studio, Toronto. A great addition to any Canadiana library.

Shea's Hippodrome was on the west side of Teraulay (later Bay) Street north of Queen. The site is now occupied by a portion of Nathan Phillips Square. On the marquee in late October 1941 ... *Citizen Cane.*

On a happier note, today is also the anniversary of the opening of one of Toronto's largest and most popular vaudeville houses. While the Shea brothers, Mike and Jerry, who were from Buffalo, New York, had operated a Shea's Theatre on Yonge Street in our city for many years, it was quite small when compared with the huge, almost 2,400-seat Hippodrome that brother Mike built on the west side of Teraulay Street, opposite the still relatively new City Hall, in 1914.

Today the name Teraulay no longer appears on any city map. It was in fact the extension of Bay Street north of Queen. When city officials decided to streamline the Bay and Queen intersection in 1917, the Bay and Teraulay thoroughfares were connected by cutting across a portion of lawn of today's Old City Hall. At the same time the former Teraulay name was abandoned with the entire street becoming Bay. Incidentally, the word Teraulay was a made-up term using portions of the surnames of two families, the Hayters and the McCauleys, who lived in the Yonge–Bay–Queen area in the early days of our city.

While Shea's Hippodrome began as a vaudeville house (one of the most frequent performers at Shea's was Red Skelton), it soon added moving pictures to the playbill. In its latter years it was strictly a movie theatre, albeit a very large one. Records indicate the two most popular films seen at the "Hip" were *Buck Privates* with Abbott and Costello and Elvis Presley's *Love Me Tender*. Shea's Hippodrome closed at the end of December 1956, and was demolished soon thereafter. A large portion of the old theatre site is now covered by the east side of Nathan Phillips Square.

April 27, 2008

Touring Motel Alley

A couple of weeks ago I hosted a sightseeing tour of our city, and as part of the tour I arranged for the bus to wander west along Lake Shore Boulevard through the former communities of Mimico and New Toronto before heading north on Islington to our lunch stop at the Old Mill on the Humber River.

For those who have not travelled along this part of Toronto's western waterfront lately, the changes have been astounding, especially through an area long known as "the motel strip." For years, the south side of Lake Shore Boulevard, westerly from the Humber River, was lined with an array of motels. Today only a couple are still in business, with all the others replaced by, you guessed it, condominium towers.

Even before there were motels, Humber Bay was the place where Torontonians of a century and more ago would visit to get away from the hustle, bustle, and heat of the big city. In the 1870s John Duck's Tavern provided not only overnight accommodations, but fine dining, outdoor entertainment, and yes, even a small zoo. Some years later several small entrepreneurs began offering canoes for rent at boathouses located along the banks of the Humber. For half-a-dollar courting couples could quietly paddle their way all the way up river to the ruins of William Gamble's "old mill" where a nearby snack bar offered ice cream floats for a nickel.

In the early years of the twentieth century the Lakeshore Road west of the city was simply a narrow dirt path skirting the shoreline of Lake

Ontario. With the arrival of the "horseless carriage" traffic began to increase, eventually forcing provincial officials to make some improvements to the rather rudimentary, though busy, highway. By 1917 the stretch between Toronto and Hamilton had been rebuilt, becoming the first concrete highway in the country and, as such, quickly became a popular route for motorists wishing to visit the provincial capital. Toronto-bound tourist traffic increased even more with the completion of the new Queen Elizabeth Way in the late 1930s. American visitors were especially impressed with our "QEW," with many believing the letters ER on the highway's light standards honoured their very own Eleanor Roosevelt. (The letters actually stood for "Elizabeth Regina," King George VI's wife and the person for whom the highway was named ... but let's not spoil it for them.)

To provide this huge influx of visitors with a less expensive alternative to staying in city hotels several "motor courts" (in reality, a grouping of small wooden cabins with just the basics in amenities) sprang up on the western outskirts of the city. These were the forerunners of the more modern "motor-hotels" (or motels as they became known) that over time would become a feature of the stretch of Lakeshore Road through Mimico.

One of the most interesting of these new tourist conveniences appeared in summer of 1951 with the opening of Louis Epstein's new Sunnyside Motor Hotel. While there were already several motor-hotels across the border in Etobicoke Township, the Sunnyside Motor Hotel would be the largest and the first to be opened in the city proper.

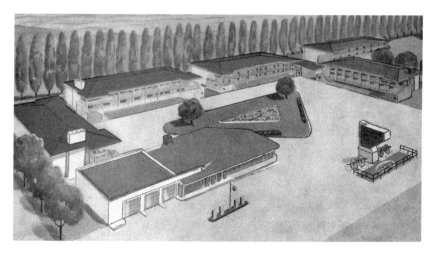

The Sunnyside Motor Hotel, which was located just east of the Humber River on the north side of Lake Shore Boulevard, is credited with being Toronto's first "motor-hotel."

Above: Brooker's drive-in restaurant can be seen at the
extreme left in this 1941 photo.
Behind it, and on the west bank
of the Humber River, is the Palace
Pier dance hall. In the foreground
is the old Humber Hotel on the
south side of what was still called
the Lakeshore Road.

Left: Brookers Lane runs south
off Lake Shore Boulevard, just
west of the Humber River. Its
name recalls Olive Brooker and
her popular drive-in restaurant.

Located on the north side of Lake Shore Boulevard West, just east
of the Humber River, it featured fifty self-contained suites, ten with
housekeeping facilities, parking spaces for all guests, a restaurant and
lunch counter, and a twenty-four-hour British-American gasoline and
service station.

As we continued our bus tour along Lake Shore Boulevard I noticed the presence of a new street sign announcing Brookers Lane, a short thoroughfare running south to the lake. Now, regular readers will be aware of my interest in the reasons why streets are called what they are. In this case, the name recalls a small drive-in restaurant called Brooker's Bar-B-Que that stood just west of the Palace Pier dance hall. Brooker's was famous for its twelve-inch hot dogs, freshly cooked, and French fries and a parking lot from which many young couple watched the submarine races.

My wife (to be) and I knew Brooker's in its latter days when it was operated by Teddy Louie and his family. Teddy and Mrs. Teddy now run the China Town take-out place on Jane Street. Back then I didn't know anything about the origins of the term Brooker's. However, a recent search of the old Telegram newspaper revealed that Olive M. Brooker was the original owner of the restaurant. According to one article, Olive's real claim to fame is that she was the person who introduced the term "Bar-B-Que" to Torontonians.

May 4, 2008

What's in a Name?

I previously wrote about Shea's Hippodrome, a huge building that opened in 1914 as a vaudeville house at 18 Teraulay Street and closed forty-four years later as a movie house at 440-448 Bay Street. No, the landmark building hadn't been relocated. Rather the street on which it had stood for all those years had simply been renamed. And that was done when city officials decided to connect Bay Street (that ran from the waterfront to Queen Street) with Teraulay Street (that ran from Queen north to College Street). What had been two separate streets then became one north-south thoroughfare with the connecting link

Courtesy of the City of Toronto Archives.

Bay Street looking south from Dundas Street West, 1954. Note the large Eaton factories in the left background, a trio of PCC streetcars on the Dupont route (abandoned when the University subway opened in 1963), and a futuristic-looking Studebaker turning from Bay onto Dundas.

still visible as the curved stretch that cuts across the lawn of today's Old City Hall.

Since my column appeared I've had several notes from readers saying that they remembered another Teraulay Street, one that ran between Yonge and Bay Streets just south of Dundas. They were right, although that particular Teraulay was the second with that name. It disappeared with the construction of the new Eaton Centre in the mid-1970s.

In the scheme of things, the name "Teraulay" is one of the oldest place names in the history of our community. In its original context it was the name of Dr. James Macaulay's residence, a place he called Teraulay Cottage. The doctor was a surgeon in a British regiment commanded by John Graves Simcoe, the future Province of Upper Canada's first lieutenant governor. Simcoe and Macaulay had both seen action during the American Revolutionary War and had become fast friends. Following Simcoe's appointment as head of the new province, the governor requested that the doctor join his Queen's Rangers as its regimental surgeon.

Similar view today. Streetcars were removed from this part of Bay Street in 1975 coinciding with the start of construction of the new Eaton Centre. Just south of the new Canadian Tire store is the Marriott Hotel. The Toronto Hydro building across from this hotel is still known as the Teraulay Transformer Station.

As an army officer, one of the perks Macaulay received was a selection of land grants. In 1797, he received what would become the most important one of all. Identified as Lot 9, this particular 100-acre parcel of land was located on the west side of today's Yonge Street stretching from Queen Street (then called Lot Street because of the lots that fronted on it) north to what we now know as Bloor Street. It was on this property that he built a house one he named Teraulay Cottage. The doctor created that unusual name by combining portions of his own surname with a few letters from his wife's maiden name. She was Elizabeth Hayter.

Years later, Macaulay's property was subdivided and a selection of streets laid out. Three of these, James, Edward, and Elizabeth, were named in recognition of Macaulay family members and are still there. Others, including Hayter, Anne, and Louisa, have all disappeared under the Eaton Centre.

Gone, too, is the original Teraulay Street, but not without a fight. To placate the history buffs of the day, Alice Street, a short thoroughfare situated one south of Dundas and running between Yonge and the newly named Bay Street, was given the name Teraulay. But it too disappeared, buried under the north end of the Eaton Centre.

The historic Church of the Holy Trinity stands on land donated by the Macaulay family.

May 11, 2008

Safety Back in the Day

With the long weekend upon us and summer just around the corner, there's a noticeable increase in the number of cars and trucks on city streets and provincial highways. Amongst those thousands of drivers there'll be speeders and they'll cause accidents, many of which will have tragic consequences, and not just for those who speed.

Motorcycles were used as early as 1912 to assist with traffic control. Here Dennis Draper, who served as police chief from 1928–1946, poses with members of his motorcycle squad on Dundas Street west of Yonge.

In what often seems a losing crusade, the Ontario Provincial Police's Cam Wooley and his colleagues continue to counsel drivers to belt up and slow down so that everyone will be able to enjoy a nice, long, accident-free season.

Actually, what prompts this particular column was a report I came across in a Toronto newspaper. The heading that caught my attention read "Fatal Bronte Crash Best Argument for Safety Belts." The story went on to describe a head-on crash on the Queen Elizabeth Highway just west of Oakville in which there were fatalities. According to the provincial police officer attending the accident, if the victims had been wearing what were described by the reporter as "passenger safety belts" it was quite likely that the deaths could have been avoided. Why had he made that assumption? Because there had been minimal structural damage to the vehicles. The fatalities actually resulted from the victims being thrown about inside the cars before being ejected onto the pavement resulting in additional injuries that were to prove fatal.

A recent story, you ask? Nope. That newspaper was dated November 14, 1952 ... more than a half-century ago!

In this photo taken in the fall of 1952, an officer with the Township of Etobicoke Police Department keeps an eye on Highway 27 traffic south of Malton Airport. Things got particularly busy when workers, who were building the CF-100 jet fighter, changed shifts at the Avro Canada factory.

The officer, when interviewed further by the reporter, offered a few suggestions as to what items he thought would help reduce the severity of accidents. Back in 1952, seat belts were not available even as an option. In fact, only racing car drivers had them. Nevertheless, the officer felt that lap, or better still, shoulder harnesses would be the most effective way to cut down on injuries. Dual or even triple braking systems would also help, as would safety tire rims that lessened the chance of losing control when a tire blew out. Headlights that automatically dimmed to prevent drivers of approaching cars being blinded and losing control of their vehicle, the use of "pop-out" windshields, and padded dashes and steering wheels were other features the OPP officer felt the car companies should incorporate in all new vehicles. Even something as simple as push button-type door handles that would lessen the chance of car doors flying open (as they often did even in a minor accident) would be a step forward.

A year or so after this story appeared in the old "Tely," details about the OPP's new weapon against speeding began appearing in the media. That weapon was identified as a "radar speedometer." It was set up on May 26, 1954, on the Queen Elizabeth Highway one mile west of the Humber River. However, unlike today the presence of the radar was plainly identified by a large sign placed several hundred feet in front of the unit.

In an interview following the experiment, the first of its kind in the country, OPP Commissioner E.V. McNeill made it clear that the police didn't want to throw a lot of tickets at drivers; they just wanted to get the speed down. Interesting concept.

One month later the first person caught speeding in a "radar speed trap" settled out of court. The fine ... $17.

May 17, 2008

* Cam Wooley is now an on-air personality with CP24 Television.

Swimmingly Good Times

I see that former Toronto mayor David Crombie has been given more time to try and come up with a solution to the Toronto District School Board's decision to close a number of school swimming pools. It's been suggested that without additional funding the plug will have to be pulled on at least twenty pools by the end of June. The story gets even worse. Without an infusion of money from either the private or public sector (or both) officials warn that by this time next year twice that number of school swimming facilities will sit, dare I say it, "high and dry."

Interestingly, swimming has always been a popular pastime here in our city. Take, for instance, this sports story I came across in the August 25, 1924, *Evening Telegram*. It dealt with the fact that a new record had been set in what was known as the annual "Gap-to-Gap" swim. In this case, the gaps mentioned in the title of the event were the East Gap and the West Gap, the channels that lead into and out of Toronto Harbour.

The swimmer who set the new record was none other than fourteen-year-old George Young who covered the two mile, eighty yard distance in fifty-four minutes, a full forty-two seconds faster than the standing record that had been set the previous year. Some readers may recognize the winner's name for it was the same Toronto-born George Young who went on to win the 1927 Wrigley Ocean Marathon, covering the twenty-two miles between the California mainland and Catalina Island in fifteen hours, forty-four minutes.

A virtual unknown until his Wrigley success, "the Catalina Kid" returned to his hometown where he received a welcome not seen since world champion oarsman and Toronto native Ned Hanlan made his triumphal return decades before. George died in obscurity in 1972, and many years would pass before he was finally recognized and inducted into Canada's Sports Hall of Fame.

Another interesting connection our city has with swimming was the "Free Bathing Car." It was the belief of R.J. Fleming, the general manager of the Toronto Railway Company (predecessor to our beloved TTC) that every child should be able to swim. To that end, Fleming's company persuaded the city to provide free lessons at four different locations: Sunnyside, on the Don River, at Fisherman's Island (near today's East Gap), and at the Western sandbar (now the site of the airport on Toronto Island). To make this arrangement work the streetcar company provided a number of streetcars that would roam various routes, picking up youngsters, and conveying them to and from the various locations free of charge; thus the term "Free Bathing Car." This unique summertime service was continued by the TTC after its creation in 1921 and continued for almost three more decades.

There's one other city landmark that had a definite connection with the popularity of swimming here in Toronto. The High Park

Hundreds of children took advantage of the TTC's "Free Bathing Cars" to get them to and from the Sunnyside bathing beaches. This photo is from the TTC Archives and is dated 1924.

Courtesy of the City of Toronto Archives.

Dr. William McCormick's sanatorium looms over the High Park "Minnies." While the mineral baths are gone, the building, now beautifully restored, is still standing at 32 Gothic Avenue. Bloor Street is behind the photographer.

Mineral Baths were located on the north side of Bloor Street opposite High Park. This facility, too, was the creation of a man who believed every child should be able to swim.

Dr. William McCormick was the owner of a sanatorium which occupied a large house that had been built in 1889 on a hill north of and overlooking Bloor Street by a former Town of West Toronto Junction alderman and mayor, George St. Jean Leger. The doctor constructed a pair of outdoor baths for his patients that were said to be naturally supplied with health-giving mineral spring waters. These baths (that by now had become known far and wide as simply "the Minnies") were eventually opened to the general public.

Dr. McCormick eventually closed his sanatorium and the building was converted into a private care facility known as the Strathcona Hospital. This landmark structure is now a key part of the Gothic Estates, an unique residential property at 32 Gothic Avenue.

The "Minnies" continued to be a popular place to swim until the construction of the Keele to Islington extension of the Bloor-Danforth subway forced their closure in the mid-1960s.

May 25, 2008

Gas Price Wars Revisited

Every once in a while a thoughtful reader will drop off something that they think I'll find of interest from an historical point-of-view. Recently a bundle of old Toronto newspapers, with my name on the wrapper, appeared in the *Sun's* mail room.

While I don't usually find out-of-date newspapers all that interesting, I spied one edition that did peak my curiosity. On the front page of the issue dated June 3, 1958, the headline "Fill Tanks with 31.9 Cent Gas" jumped off the page. With gasoline prices the topic of just about any conversation these days I just had to read the article, as ancient as it was.

First let me remind those who are not of the Imperial measurement era that the 31.9 cents in the headline wasn't for a litre (even though that would have been a good deal), but for a gallon. And not just the puny American-type gallon either, but our very own Imperial gallon. Some deft calculating using the slide rule that got me through Ryerson told me that 31.9 cents an Imperial gallon works out to something like 7 cents a litre. An unfair comparison, no question, since the papers were 10 cents and a five-room house in North Toronto was just $14,900. Nevertheless, one can reminisce, can't one?

Another interesting fact about gas stations and gas wars in the Toronto of 50 years ago has to do with the number of different brands available to the motorists back then. Let me paraphrase a paragraph or two from that June 3, 1958, article:

Fifty years ago gasoline price wars were common in Toronto. On March 24, 1958, this Imperial station at the corner of Dundas and Church Streets in downtown Toronto was selling regular gas for 36.9 cents a gallon. The normal price was 43.9. That's old Mutual Street Arena (the original home of the Maple Leaf hockey team) in the background.

Photo by Yarmila Filey.

Until the early 1980s, the term Imperial Esso was a common site on hundreds of gas stations across Canada. Slowly the term Imperial began to vanish. Interestingly, Lou's Esso service station at 1455 Royal York Road (just north of Eglinton Avenue) still retains the word "Imperial" on the front of the building.

Anyone remember this old Imperial Oil station on Toronto's Central Waterfront? The photo was taken sometime in the 1930s. Note what appears to be a popcorn wagon parked at the curb.

The latest price war among service stations along Danforth Ave., Kingston Rd., Kennedy Rd. and Gerrard St. E. has lasted two weeks and according to station operators shows signs of spreading to other parts of the Metropolitan area. The price of 31.9 cents, about 10 cents below normal was set by the operator of the Cities Service station near the Danforth and Luttrell intersection. The operator of the nearby British American station said he wasn't selling much gas at 35.9 cents. He blamed the price war on a dispute between a Shell service station and an independent company, Vigor Oil Co.

The Fina station at Victoria Park and the Danforth is selling at 33 cents a gallon as is a neighboring Texaco outlet. The Shell station on Gerrard maintained a price of 33 cents as did a nearby Sunoco station. At Warden and Danforth a Regent station and Vigor station showed gas at 33.9 while the sign in front of the Supertest outlet on the Danforth near Victoria Park showed 33 cents even.

What becomes obvious is the number of different brands. Can it be that the limited number we have to choose from today has had an effect on the price of a gallon ... er ... litre of gasoline? Just wondering.

June 1, 2008

Babe a Hit in Toronto

I watched the trio of New York Yankees–Toronto Blue Jay baseball games on TV last week. After the third game I had the strangest daydream. I was on the game show *Jeopardy* and the conversation went like this:

Alex: "Mike, what category would you like?"

Mike: "I'll take Baseball Trivia for $1,000."

Alex: "Here's the answer. It was the city in which the legendary Babe Ruth hit his first home run as a professional baseball player."

Mike: "What is Toronto?"

Alex: "Correct!"

Unfortunately, in my dream I then got all the following questions wrong and didn't make the final round. I did feel better, however, once I realized that I had left the *Jeopardy* studio audience closed-mouthed once they learned that this great American icon had hit the first of hundreds of home runs in, of all places, Canada, and more specifically in my home town. It's the same reaction I get when I tell tourists from south of the border that Mary Pickford, who was known world-wide as "America's Sweetheart," was actually born here in Toronto.

The game during which Ruth hit that special homerun took place on Saturday, September 5, 1914, at the four-year-old stadium at Hanlan's Point on the Island. The game was the first of two that afternoon and it turned out to be a romp for the Grays with the Leafs going down to defeat 9-0. Ruth pitched the nine innings striking out seven, giving up three

Heritage Toronto erected this commemorative plaque near the Hanlan's Point ferry dock on Toronto Island, a location not far from the stadium where Babe Ruth hit the first professional home run in his long baseball career. Several New York Yankees were present at the ceremony.

Newspaper ad announcing Babe Ruth's appearance in a Yankee–Maple Leaf exhibition game at Toronto's Maple Leaf Stadium at Bathurst and Fleet (now Lake Shore Boulevard West) on July 7, 1927. The "Babe" played first base while Lou Gehrig was in right field. Our guys won 11–7 then lost to their International league rivals from Reading 8–4.

This aerial view shows the stadium at Hanlan's Point on Toronto Island. It was here that Ruth hit his first professional home run with the ball sailing over the right field fence. Adjacent to the stadium was the extremely popular Maple Leaf amusement park. Its huge white wooden coaster was called "The Racer." The Island Airport would be built years later on "the sandbar" to the left of centre. Separating it from the city is the Western Channel. Across the Bay is the Dominion Shipbuilding yard located just west of the foot of Spadina Avenue.

base-on-balls. The Leafs got just one hit and that came in the first inning. Ruth also hit the game's only home run, with the ball sailing over the right field fence. Count three more runs as there were two on base.

And, as one newspaper reported, the nineteen-year-old wasn't yet old enough to vote, with twenty-five being the age of majority back then.

The second game had a better result for the hometown boys, who won it 3–2. However, it was a shortened affair since the Providence team had to catch a train in order to get home in time to play a Sunday game. That was something the Toronto players wouldn't have to worry about for decades since Sunday sports (and a lot of other things) were banned by law.

June 8, 2008

Rose by Any Other Name

It was June 18, 1910, that eight-year-old Phyllis Osler, accompanied by her grandfather Edmund Osler, president of the Toronto Ferry company, and its manager Lawrence Solman, made their way by automobile from Osler's beautiful Rosedale residence to the Polson Iron Works yard on the Toronto waterfront near the foot of Sherbourne Street. It was there that a small group of invited guests had gathered in anticipation of the launch of the ferry company's newest addition to its fleet serving the crowds visiting Toronto Island.

Shortly after noon the mandatory bottle of wine crashed against the double-ended paddle steamer's bow as the youngster christened the craft *Trillium*, a name that had been suggested by Miss Ruth Spry, the young niece of the Polson Iron Works' manager J.J. Main.

The ceremonies were no sooner over and the dignitaries and invited guests off to a special luncheon when Polson crews began swarming over the vessel. Within a few minutes the Scotch marine boiler was being lowered into place. Once that was done the pre-fabricated fore and aft cabins were bolted into place. There would be no difficulty in having *Trillium* totally fitted out and ready to join the others flowers in the fleet, *Mayflower*, *Primrose*, and *Blue Bell*, in anticipation of the expected rush to the Island on the Dominion Day holiday that was less than two weeks away.

Trillium remained in Island service for the privately-owned Toronto Ferry Company until 1927 when it and all of the company's other

In late 1973, the abandoned Toronto Island ferry *Trillium* was towed from an Island lagoon to the mainland prior to undergoing a million dollars worth of restoration. The story of the project as well as the history of Toronto Island ferry boats can be found in my book *Trillium and Toronto Island*.

Restoration took nearly two years before *Trillium* returned to service on Toronto Harbour in the spring of 1976.

An added extra to writing my column comes in the form of the unexpected appearance of great old photos such as this one from reader Bruce Baker. Here we see *Trillium* being towed to the Island in 1957 where many believed she would be "out of sight, out of mind." Note the city's tallest building of the day, the 1931 Bank of Commerce Building, dominating the skyline.

Island craft were turned over to the municipally-controlled Toronto Transportation (renamed Transit in 1954) Company. The TTC now operated streetcars, buses, and (after March, 1954) subway trains. Oh, and a small "navy" that included *Trillium*. However, by 1957 the older vessels, including *Trillium*'s sister *Blue Bell*, were worn out and set aside with the latter eventually converted into a garbage scow. Fate spared *Trillium*, and in November, 1973, after languishing in an Island lagoon for more than a decade, the council of Metropolitan Toronto approved restoring the vessel to operating condition. Gordon Champion was hired to supervise and coordinate the million-dollar project.

On December 7, 1973, the badly deteriorated vessel was towed to the mainland and a pre-inspection undertaken. Preliminary work was done at a dry dock in Oshawa, after which *Trillium* was towed across the lake and through the Welland Canal to Port Colborne where the talented crew at Fraser Marine began the task of restoring the "ancient" craft.

Late in 1975 *Trillium* returned to Toronto Harbour, and on May 19, 1976, nearly sixty-six years after Phyllis smashed that bottle of wine on the paddle wheeler's bow, *Trillium* was back in service.

Thanks to the people at Toronto Parks, Forestry and Recreation, *Trillium* will be ferrying people back and forth to Centre Island during select periods.

June 15, 2008

A Shining Example

While today's mariners often rely on a GPS to find their way, the "ancient mariners" relied on the friendly beam of light emanating from strategically placed lighthouses. In Canada there are nearly six hundred of these lonely sentinels and they come in all shapes and sizes. Ontario alone has more than one hundred, the vast majority to be found from one end of the Great Lakes system to the other. Interestingly, the oldest is right here in Toronto. Though no longer operational, the Gibraltar Point lighthouse on Toronto Island was for many decades the guiding light for ships buffeted by high seas and raked by bone chilling winds that were desperately seeking their way into the safety of Toronto Harbour.

Not long after his arrival in 1791 John Graves Simcoe the first lieutenant governor of Upper Canada recognized the need for a pair of lighthouses to assist lake travellers making their way between his capital at Newark (Niagara-on-the-Lake) and the busy harbour at the Town of York the community he had established in 1793. The governor ordered that one lighthouse be built at Mississauga Point at the mouth of the Niagara River with another on the "peninsula" (after a vicious storm in early 1858, Toronto Island). The location he chose on this side of the lake was called Gibraltar Point, a name Simcoe selected because it reminded him of the defence characteristics of Gibraltar at the entrance to the Mediterranean.

The Gibraltar Point lighthouse can be seen at the lower right in this rare aerial photo taken in 1919 from a biplane (note the plane's lower wing and a strut at the left of the view). The land reclamation in the centre background is taking place at Mugg's Island while to the west of it are the docks at the entrance to the amusement park located on a much smaller Hanlan's Point. The Island airport would be built on land still to come to the extreme left of the photo.

Construction of the original Gibraltar Point lighthouse was completed in 1808. Built of limestone hauled by barge from Queenston on the Niagara River, it stood 52 feet high. In 1832 the lighthouse was raised an extra 12 feet, this time using stone brought to the site from Kingston. At first whale oil was used as a source of illuminating the fixed light in the lantern. In 1863 cheaper coal oil was substituted for the whale oil.

Fifteen years passed before a more visible revolving light was installed. The revolving motion was accomplished using a cable with a heavy weight at one end. The cable was attached to the lamp mechanism with the other end wound around a large drum. As the weight descended through the interior of the lighthouse it pulled on the cable which in turn caused the light to rotate. It was the responsibility of the lighthouse keeper to rewind the drum every fourteen hours. In the winter of 1916–17, a fixed electric light that flashed on and off replaced the oil lamp. Before long, however, that white light became indistinguishable in amongst the myriad of city lights appearing on the changing city skyline, and a fixed green light was installed. The lighthouse was then decommissioned in 1956, its light replaced by an automatic electric signal. Two years later

The historic Gibraltar Point lighthouse was erected on Toronto Island's Lake Ontario shoreline two centuries ago.

the historic structure was transferred to the custody of the Metropolitan Toronto government. Since 1999 it has been the responsibility of the newly created City of Toronto.

No story about Toronto's historic lighthouse would be complete without reference to an event that took place on January 2, 1815. It seems that the lighthouse keeper of the day, one J. P. Rademuller, kept a substantial quantity of beer on the premises. One evening, perhaps still in a festive mood from the previous New Year's Eve, several soldiers from the fort over on the mainland stopped by for a visit. Heavy drinking ensued, and when Rademuller suggested the boys had had enough. They disagreed, violently. A confrontation ensued resulting in the demise of the lighthouse keeper. It said his remains were buried just west of his lighthouse. Is the story true? And if it is, does the ghost of Rademuller still haunt the lighthouse as it seeks justice after 193 years?

Your guess is as good as mine.

June 22, 2008

Gooderham, Worts, and All

It just doesn't seem possible that it was nearly a decade ago that I stood on the main street of the Gooderham and Worts distillery with plant manager Paul Allsop. Together we watched as the last truckload of rum to be produced at this historic site at the east end of Toronto's developing waterfront rumbled out the gate headed for the nation's west coast.

Commercial operations on this site actually got started in 1832 when partners James Worts and William Gooderham, recent immigrants from Yorkshire in England, began milling grain. However, since it was Mr. Worts who was the first of the two to arrive in York, Upper Canada, from Yorkshire, England, the enterprise was initially set up, not as today's well-known Gooderham and Worts, but rather as Worts and Gooderham. A few months later, Worts' brother-in-law William Gooderham arrived in town along with a large number of members from both families.

In 1834 the fledgling company was faced with a major crisis when James Worts, despondent following his wife's sudden death while giving birth, committed suicide by throwing himself down the company well. This left William Gooderham to carry on as the sole proprietor. He was more than equal to the task. As time passed it became obvious to Gooderham that instead of simply grinding the grain there was a lot more money to be made converting that same grain into alcohol and selling that product instead. The idea took off, and by 1845 the company was sufficiently busy for him to offer a position to his late partner's son James

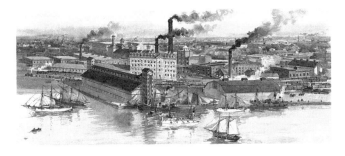

This beautifully drawn bird's eye view of the Gooderham and Worts complex was created in 1896. Note the large Stone Distillery building which is still a feature of the site.

Gooderham Worts. With his young relative now part of the enterprise a new name was adopted. It would henceforth be known as Gooderham and Worts, a title that would become known worldwide for the many liquid products produced in the complex of buildings that still stand on the grounds of what has become one of the city's newest attractions, the Historic Distillery District.

Though not on the actual distillery site itself, there is another Toronto landmark that also retains the famous Gooderham name. Not far to the west, at the intersection of Front, Church, and Wellington Streets, is the unique triangular-shaped Gooderham Building. It was erected in 1891–92 by George Gooderham who had succeeded his father when the latter died in 1881. The structure was designed by David Roberts, Jr. (whose father was the architect of the massive Stone Distillery building that still stands on the Gooderham and Worts property) and it was here

In the background of this photo is the Gooderham Building at the Church, Wellington, and Front intersection. Following its completion in 1892 it was the site of the Gooderham and Worts head office. In this 1951 photo it was just another building surrounded by wholesale warehouses and produce delivery trucks. Today it's one of Toronto's few remaining jewels.

that George would have his office and where he would look after his many business interests. These included the distillery that by now had become the largest in the world. It was rumoured that the boss would often keep a watchful eye on the goings-on at the distillery through the curved windows of his office located under the inverted cone-shaped cupola on the building's fifth floor.

In addition to Gooderham's distilling interests he was also into railroads (the Toronto and Nipissing), insurance (Manufacturers' Life), and banking (the Bank of Toronto). And in May 1903, just two years before his death, Toronto's best-known businessman and philanthropist beamed with pride at the opening of the city's newest and finest hostelry, his King Edward Hotel.

Many more stories about the Gooderham and Worts complex and its amazing transformation into today's popular Historic Distillery District can be found in a beautiful book by Sally Gibson. Illustrated with rare colour photos and sketches as well as numerous contemporary views, *Toronto's Distillery District, History by the Lake* (Cityscape Holdings, $65), covers a wide variety of topics related to the Gooderham and Worts complex, including the company's famous windmill, the devastating 1869 fire, the trials and tribulations faced during the prohibition years, and the plans (often derailed) to retain the historic site intact. The book is available in several local bookstores as well as at the Historic Distillery District.

June 29, 2008

Lights, Action, Drive!

It wasn't long after the twentieth century dawned and the first primitive automobiles began puttering along the dusty, often muddy Toronto streets that people began clamouring for city officials to enact rules and regulations to control the growing traffic problem. In fact, an editorial in a Toronto newspaper dated July 24, 1903, lays it on the line:

> The automobile has come to stay and will doubtlessly be amongst the most beneficial of modern inventions. But such vehicles cannot be entrusted to the careless and incautious. The safety of the general public demands that all reckless drivers be weeded out.

Some of the worst offenders were the "scorchers," a title that identified speeders, but not just those who were in charge of an automobile, but bicycle riders as well. Pedestrians, too, were becoming a traffic concern. With ever increasing numbers of cars and pedestrians using the downtown streets, jay-walking was become a serious problem. In fact, following a 1924 inquest into a pedestrian fatality, a suggestion was made by a coroner's jury that if approved would have seen a chain placed down the middle of busy streets such as Yonge and Queen that would eliminate jay-walking by forcing those on foot to cross only at intersections. While that proposal was obviously unworkable, Police Chief Sam Dickson

Pedestrians, cars, and streetcars get in each others' way outside the old Eaton's store on Yonge Street, circa 1944.

ordered his traffic officers to hand out cards on which the words "You are jay-walking" were written.

It wasn't until 1925 that Toronto's first real attempt to regulate the interaction of pedestrians and automobiles attempting to use the same stretch of road was tried. Officials had been keeping an eye on a new invention that had first been used in Detroit five years earlier. Things were getting so bad in our city that they decided to give this "automatic traffic signal" a try. They selected the intersection of Yonge and Bloor as the test site. Up until now hand operated traffic semaphores had been used at this and other corners when things got particularly busy. But, these portable units had several drawbacks. First, it was dangerous for the officers standing in the middle of a busy intersection with vehicles speeding by in all directions. It was even worse in inclement weather when the officer and semaphore became almost invisible. This type of signal device was also highly inefficient, requiring as it did an officer who had more important police work that he could, and in many cases should, be doing.

The Toronto trial featured a set of four "automatic traffic signals" with one signal facing in each direction. Each signal consisted of three coloured

Courtesy of TTC Archives.

A police officer keeps traffic moving at the Yonge and Bloor intersection with the aid of a traffic semaphore, circa 1915. Note the wagonload of hay southbound on Yonge, while beside the traffic officer a city worker cleans up some "used" hay.

lamps: red, amber and green. Interestingly, each signal was positioned horizontally, unlike the modern day vertical installation. Control of the signals was set to "automatic" (although they could be controlled manually) which meant that the Yonge Street traffic (vehicles and pedestrians) would get a green light and be able to proceed for thirty seconds while the Bloor traffic was held by a red light. The amber light would then illuminate for three seconds, after which the Bloor Street traffic would get a green light while the Yonge was held by the red. The sequence would then be repeated. In the event of an emergency a police officer could override the system and turn all the lights red for as long as necessary to permit fire trucks or ambulances to get through the intersection quickly.

The trial only lasted for a short time based on the fact that in photos showing the same intersection the following year the manually-operated traffic semaphore is back in use.

The next we hear of the automatic traffic signals project is when a newspaper report appearing on March 11, 1927, advises that the signals are now in operation at the Yonge and Queen corner and "will soon be turned on all the way down to King Street."

The new setup was installed vertically (as traffic lights are today), and though the red and green lights were present the amber light was missing.

Toronto saw electric traffic signals for the first time on August 8, 1925. The signals were installed on a trial basis at this same Yonge and Bloor intersection. Note that the very first signals were installed horizontally.

To signify that the signals were about to change, all the lamps went dark for three seconds. (Bet that was fun!) The middle lamp would flash red to stop all traffic from entering the intersection in the event of an emergency.

Since those trial-and-error days there have been numerous changes to the city's traffic signal system. I can remember when the lights at some of the less busy signalized intersections were turned off at night and when the green and amber lights came on together. One of the best things they did from a safety standpoint was to make the whole intersection red for a few seconds. Before that you could anticipate the red turning to green and cruise through the intersection without even slowing down.

By the way, from that first set of experimental signals at Yonge and Bloor, any idea how many signalized intersections there are throughout the city today? Exactly 2,098 with the most recent activated last Thursday. And the cost of signalizing each intersection? Approximately $130,000.

July 6, 2008

Our Changing Skyline

Today, when we talk about the amazing changes Toronto has undergone over a relatively short period of time, one way to confirm this statement is to simply view the trio of photographs accompanying this column. All were all taken from approximately the same location on Toronto Bay, and each one captures the skyline of the day.

1922: Scanning the photo from left (west) to right (east) we see Union Station (virtually complete, but due to ongoing problems with the location of the railway tracks still not open to the public). In front of it, and sitting

Toronto skyline, circa 1922.

Similar view, nine years later.

right on the water's edge, is the Toronto Harbour Commission Building. Erected in 1917–18, in 1999 it became the home of the Toronto Port Authority and the Harbour 60 restaurant. Rising above all is the 300-foot-high clock tower of the twenty-four-year-old City Hall at the Queen Street corner. Next along the water's edge are the numerous ferries (including *Trillium*) that served Toronto Island. Moving east we see three of Toronto's early "skyscrapers" — Dominion Bank, Royal Bank, and the CPR building — standing at the Yonge and King intersection. All three are still there. In the foreground, at the foot of Yonge Street, are several of the passenger boats that carried thousands to various Lake Ontario ports.

1931: Moving from left to right we see the two-year-old Royal York Hotel and in the foreground the new Union Station that with the railway viaduct finally in place had opened early the previous year. Several of the new sheds built to serve the increasing number of lake freighters calling at the Port of Toronto and erected on land reclaimed from the harbour are also visible. Looking north on Bay Street we can still see the clock tower of City Hall. Piercing the skyline is the new Bank of Commerce Building, its top floor still encased in scaffolding. At 463 feet and thirty-four floors, the structure was not only the tallest in the city, but for many years the tallest in what was still referred to as the British Commonwealth. Now known as Commerce Court North, it remains as one of Toronto's most magnificent skyscrapers. The pioneer high rise buildings at Yonge and King are still visible as is the 1921–22 addition to the King Edward Hotel. At the extreme right of the view is the spire of the Cathedral of St. James which was completed in 1875 and remained the highest point in the entire city for many years. The large twin-stack vessel in the foreground is the S.S. *Kingston*, one of several large Lake Ontario passenger ships whose home port was Toronto.

The view today.

2008: The present day Toronto skyline is dominated by condominium towers, hotels, and bank buildings. Among the latter is First Canadian Place (the white structure visible above the ferry boat, completed in 1975) which towers nearly 984 feet above the King and Bay intersection and is the tallest building in the country. Crossing in the foreground is the Toronto Island ferry *Thomas Rennie* that entered service in 1951 and was named in recognition of a prominent city businessman who was also a long-time Toronto Harbour Commissioner.

July 20, 2008

On the Waterfront

Featured in the previous column was a trio of photographs taken from approximately the same location on Toronto Bay. They showed the remarkable changes in the city's skyline over a period of eighty-five years. I've selected three more waterfront views, although this time rather than being photos of the whole skyline they focus specifically on the foot of Yonge Street. Here we go:

Looking north from Toronto Bay towards the dock at the foot of Yonge Street. When this photo was taken in 1928 the Metropolitan Building (seen over the word TIRE) was the tallest structure in the city.

1926: For many years this would be the view that visitors arriving in Toronto by passenger ship would get as their vessel docked at or near the foot of Yonge Street. Although this photo was snapped in the dead of winter and the slip is full of ice, the warmer weather scene was very different as hundreds of people made their way into the city over badly maintained wooden sidewalks then had to navigate a dozen or so railway tracks that crossed Yonge Street at The Esplanade. Frequently there'd be a freight or passenger train straddling the crossing, forcing luggage-laden pedestrians to either wait until the train moved or try their luck squeezing between the individual cars. Over the years there were several unfortunate incidents where pedestrians were maimed or even killed trying to get past the trains. In fact, it was the seriousness of the situation that helped get the cross-waterfront railway viaduct built.

A remnant of those early railway days can be seen in the photo. The structure with the curved roof and located just east of the Yonge and The Esplanade train crossing was built in 1866 as a station for the pioneer Great Western Railway. It later became a wholesale fruit market and burned in 1952. Eight years later the O'Keefe (later the Hummingbird, now the Sony) Centre opened on the site.

The trio of skyscrapers on Yonge Street are at the Yonge and King intersection (all of which still stand), while the fourth is the former Traders Bank at northeast corner of Yonge and Colborne Streets. It and the Metropolitan Building (at the southwest corner of Adelaide and Victoria and over the Dominion Tires sign) had the distinction of being the tallest buildings in the city when each opened, the former in 1905, the latter exactly twenty years later. To the extreme right of the view is the 1921–22 addition to the King Edward Hotel.

Of particular interest is the fact that the photo shows just how far inland the waters of Toronto Bay once came.

1935: With the completion of the cross-waterfront railway viaduct in the late 1920s a couple of things finally became possible. First, the long-delayed Union Station could open and begin to serve the train-travelling public, and second, important north–south thoroughfares such as York, Bay, and Yonge could be extended south to connect with Queen's Quay, which had been laid out across the city's newly reclaimed waterfront.

In this view we see the recently constructed and paved Yonge Street just north of its intersection with Queen's Quay. On the skyline (left) is the 1931 Bank of Commerce Building (now Commerce Court North), its

This 1935 photo looks north up a newly extended and paved Yonge Street towards the recently completed railway underpass. The 1866 Great Western railway station seen in the first photo is still visible.

Looking north from the bay towards the Yonge Street slip. The sailboat adds a little calmness to a busy photograph.

towering thirty-four story height making it the tallest building in the city, country, and British Commonwealth.

The white structure on the west side of Yonge just north of the railway viaduct is the Dominion Public Building. Situated on the south side of Front between Yonge and Bay it was built in two phases with the first opening in 1926, the second in 1935.

The Yonge and King skyscrapers are still there as is the King Eddy addition. To the extreme right of the photo is the 1875 spire of St. James Cathedral. When completed the spire was the highest object on the skyline. To help Lake Ontario mariners that were searching in the dark for the Port of Toronto find their way, officials ordered that a light be placed in the spire.

2008: This modern-day view, looking north up Yonge Street from Toronto Bay, is crowded with condo towers, hotels, and office buildings. In the slip at the foot of Yonge is Captain John's floating restaurant. The MS *Jadran* originally operated as a seven hundred passenger cruise boat on the Adriatic, Black, and Aegean Seas, arriving in our city after Captain John Letnik purchased the vessel from the Yugoslavian government in 1975. Further up Yonge Street is the Gardiner Expressway, the railway underpass, and the Yonge and King "skyscrapers" that are also visible in the two earlier photos.

July 27, 2008

Hooray, Simcoe Day

It's that time again, time to debunk the myth that the Simcoe Day holiday was originally named to honour a Japanese car. In fact, the title of this long-time mid-summer holiday was somewhat more elaborate than the simple Civic Holiday by which it became known. Let me quote the official proclamation that appeared in the Toronto newspapers on August 1, 1870:

> To all whom these Presents may Concern:
>
> Whereas for years past the Council of the Corporation of the City of Toronto has set apart one day as a Public Holiday to be observed for the recreation and amusement of the Citizens and to be known as the "Citizens' Annual Holiday",
>
> And whereas the Council for the present year and in order continue this good and proper consideration for the health and happiness of the Citizens has by Resolution set apart Monday the 8th day of August as the Citizens' Annual Holiday for the year 1870.
>
> And in order that all parties may have an opportunity of enjoying themselves on that day the citizens are requested to close all places of business.

In witness thereof I have caused this proclamation to be made public at Toronto, this 1st day of August, AD 1870.

George D'Arcy Boulton
President of Council

From this announcement it would appear that the summer holiday idea had been around for a while and it wasn't until 1870 that City Council gave it a specific day on which it was to be held. At first the holiday, which started officially as the "Citizens' Annual Holiday," a term that was soon simplified to "Civic Holiday," was held on the second Monday (August 8) of the month. Over the following years the holiday continued to be held on the second Monday, although for a few years in the 1880s the date for the holiday was for some unknown reason changed to the *last* Monday in August. However, that didn't last very long and it soon reverted back to the second Monday of the month.

Photo courtesy the Ontario Heritage Trust.

John Graves Simcoe's monument is just east of the Parliament Buildings. It was unveiled in 1903.

The change in timing to the first Monday in August occurred in 1897. In that year the holiday was held on August 2. And while the first Monday in August continues to be a holiday, its title (at least here in Toronto as well as in a few other communities) has been changed to Simcoe Day.

The change occurred following a suggestion made in December, 1968 by the then provincial Minister of Tourism James Auld. He believed that all Ontarians should recognize the province's first lieutenant governor, John Graves Simcoe, by altering the non-descript Civic Holiday term to Simcoe Day.

Toronto acted quickly on the minister's suggestion and within a few months city council, led by Mayor William Dennison, decreed that effective August 4, 1969, the long-standing Civic Holiday would be celebrated as Simcoe Day.

Here in Toronto, in addition to recognizing Ontario's first lieutenant governor and the founder of our community in the title of the holiday, we also have the John Graves Simcoe monument. It was unveiled on May 27, 1903, and is located just to the east of the Ontario Parliament Buildings. The work is the creation of Walter Allward whose best known work is the spectacular Vimy Ridge Memorial in France. There are also two downtown city streets, John and Simcoe, that honour the man as well as a TTC subway station on the Bloor-Danforth line that recognizes the name of Simcoe's summer home. "Castle Frank," which had been constructed in the mid-1790s high above the west bank of the Don River just north of today's Bloor Street, was in a remote location well to the north of Simcoe's small town site that he called York. It was called "Castle Frank" after Simcoe's son Francis and was to serve for several years as Simcoe's country residence. Some historians believe that the path the Governor followed as he made his way between the original Parliament Buildings on the waterfront and his summer place up the Don evolved into today's Parliament Street.

Francis Simcoe died at the age of just twenty-three during one of the fiercest battles in Spanish Peninsular War. The house was accidentally burned in 1829.

Simcoe returned to England in 1796, and ten years later passed away. His remains, along with those of his wife Elizabeth and six of their eleven children, rest within Wolford Chapel which is located near Honiton in Devon. In 1966 the chapel along with its collection of antique furnishings,

Wolford Chapel, near Honiton in Devon, England, is the final resting place of our province's first lieutenant governor.

decorative artwork, and surrounding parcel of land were donated to the people of Ontario in 1966. In 1982 the Ontario Heritage Trust assumed ownership and continue to encourage all Canadians visiting England to visit the chapel and learn more about the man we honour on Simcoe Day.

August 3, 2008

TTC Testing LRT Bidders

If Toronto is to remain a "streetcar city," as it has been since the very first tracks were laid down in 1861, its aging fleet of 248 light rail vehicles will soon have to be replaced. In a bid to acquire 204 state-of-the-art LRTs (Light Rail Vehicles), with a promise of more to come, the TTC has been seeking bids from companies in the LRT manufacturing business. Things were progressing well until it was determined that some of the specifications in the proposal submitted by Bombardier, the Canadian company that was expected to win the contract, were non-compliant. One area that failed to meet the TTC's requirements was the inability of the proposed vehicle to ascend the eight percent grade found on Bathurst Street north of Davenport Road with full traction. Another concern was the fact that the proposed Bombardier vehicles could not negotiate some of the tight curves found throughout the system, the tightest being the loop at Queen and Kingston Road.

Reports emanating from both the TTC and Bombardier (and perhaps some other companies) indicate these problems are being studied and hopefully will be addressed. Stay tuned.

*   *   *

In a somewhat transit-related matter the city is proposing to try what some claim is a new method to alleviate the vehicle versus pedestrian congestion problem that frequently occurs at the Yonge and Dundas intersection. If

In the mid-1970s it was decided that the streetcar in Toronto would be abandoned. Citizen pressure resulted in the TTC changing its mind, but that meant that new streetcars would be needed. In this view one of the 196 new Canadian Light Rail Vehicles arrives at the TTC Hillcrest Shops in April, 1979.

the experiment, which is scheduled to begin in September, is successful, it's proposed that three other busy intersections, Bay and Dundas, Yonge and Bloor, and Bay and Front, get the same treatment. However, they won't be altered until the pilot program is proven to be successful.

The plan is to make the Yonge and Dundas corner a "scramble intersection" by doing the following. The existing traffic light sequence will be altered by adding an additional phase. During the first phase vehicles only will cross east-west while pedestrians stay put. During the second phase, vehicles only will cross north-south, again pedestrians must wait. Finally, in the third phase all the lights controlling vehicles will turn red while the pedestrians signals are activated allowing the masses to cross in any direction north, south, and even diagonally. It will be Toronto's first "scramble intersection."

While the name may be new, the concept is not. Back in June of 1954, a similar attempt to improve the flow of vehicle and pedestrian traffic was introduced at the Bay and Richmond intersection. This time, however, it was called the "Barnes Dance" in recognition of its prime supporter American traffic engineer, Henry A. Barnes. The Barnes Dance was tried

One of the many streetcars built in the Toronto Railway Company car building shops on Front Street near Sherbourne negotiates the Bathurst Street hill just north of Davenport Road in 1931. At eight percent, this is the steepest grade in the city's track system and it is still a concern for the TTC.

in Denver, New York City, Vancouver, and even as far away as Melbourne, Australia. Here in Toronto, and using the same principles as will be introduced at the Yonge and Dundas corner next month, the experiment began on June 21, 1954, and was abolished less than four months later thereby suffering the same fate as every other Barnes Dance installation.

There were several reasons cited for this failure, the prime one being the impediment to the flow of vehicle traffic through the intersection. Cars still came first. One politician suggested the next trial take place in the middle of Mount Pleasant Cemetery.

I guess the question is will the Dance/Scramble experiment fare any better this time around?

August 10, 2008

*A bid from Bombardier for 204 new LRT vehicles has since been accepted, and the new vehicles can be expected in 2012.
**There are now two scramble walkways, with the newest opened on October 9, 2009, at the Yonge and Bloor intersection.

Ex Marks the Spot

It's that time again; time to visit the good old CNE as millions of Torontonians and visitors to our city have done each summer since the very first fair (originally called the Toronto Industrial Exhibition) opened in 1879.

When I was a kid, in addition to touring the midway and the numerous outdoor exhibits, it was mandatory to visit the hundreds of displays in the various exhibition buildings. I can recall the fascinating displays of arts, crafts, and hobbies in the building just inside the Dufferin Gate identified naturally enough as the Arts, Crafts and Hobbies Building. Today this building, which was actually built in 1912 as the British Governments Building, no longer houses displays but rather is home to Medieval Times.

Just to the south is the beautiful Ontario Government Building, which opened in 1926. Here I remember seeing creatures from the province's many forests and lakes. Oh, and one year they had a huge likeness of Paul Bunyan and his blue ox Babe, both constructed out of papier-mâché. Like its neighbour across the way, this once-popular exhibition building has also been closed to the public and is now the Liberty Grand, a beautiful venue for wedding receptions, book launches, and the like.

The 1907 Horticulture Building no longer has displays of horticulture while the Music Building (originally built in 1908 as a place to display the

This aerial view of the east end of the CNE was taken sometime around 1940. It shows the Electrical and Engineering Building on the north side of Princes' Boulevard, which stood where the Direct Energy Building is today. Opposite it is the Automotive Building that is presently being converted into a mammoth conference centre. Also visible is the huge Dance Tent where the big bands of the day performed during the annual fair. To the extreme right of the view is the Princes' Gates, while to the left of the photo is Stanley Barracks — a complex of buildings built to protect Toronto following the American invasion of our community in 1813. Known originally as the "New Fort," it was later renamed Stanley Barracks to honour the governor general of the day Sir Frederick Arthur Stanley and the man who donated that illusive (for Toronto anyway) hockey trophy. Only one building in the complex, the Officers' Quarters, still stands. It is to be hoped that if and when plans are finalized for a new hotel to serve the new conference centre that this ancient landmark will find a place in the development.

wonders of Canada's trio of transcontinental railways) doesn't feature the sound of music any more.

The 1961 Hockey Hall of Fame (later Canada's Sports Hall of Fame) has vanished as has the massive Grandstand that sixty years ago began featuring such diverse attractions as car stunt shows, military tattoos, and dozens of well-known entertainers such as Victor Borge, Roy Rogers, and Frank Sinatra.

Continuing as public buildings during the CNE are the Better Living Centre (1964), Queen Elizabeth Building (1957), and the Food Building (1954), with the latter (naturally enough) being the fair's most popular building.

Not far away, the Horse Palace (1931), Coliseum (1922), and Direct Energy Centre (1997) are also open to the public during the CNE.

There is, however, another long-time Exhibition building that will no longer be a part of the eighteen-day event. The Automotive Building is presently undergoing renovations to the tune of nearly $25 million which will convert the historic structure into what's referred to in the industry as a "Class A" trade show and conference centre.

The Automotive Building was officially opened on August 26, 1929, by Ontario's premier of the day, Howard Ferguson. For the next thirty-three years (thanks to the war there was no annual fair during the years 1942–46) the newest models of cars and trucks were featured attractions in the million dollar building.

Interestingly, during the new building's early years, car shows had become so popular that officials decided to hold two such shows each year, one in the spring and the other during the CNE. Both editions were held in the Automotive Building. Over the years the CNE car show became so popular that Ford decided to unveil its new Edsel to the entire world not somewhere in the States and not even on television, but at the 1957 edition of the CNE.

Then when officials decided to move the opening of the annual fair into mid-August (the CNE originally opened in early September), the only cars available for display were those that the public had already seen throughout the previous year. This fact resulted in the last "new" car show being held in the Automotive Building in 1967. From then on the place was home to a multitude of themed subjects and a variety of displays. There was even a time when the building was converted into a farm, prompting CNE people to dub it the Auto-MOO-tive Building.

August 17, 2008

Red Rockets of Yesteryear

One of the most interesting newsletters to which I subscribe is the Toronto Transportation Society's "Transfer Points." The publication is always full of interesting items on a wide variety of streetcar, bus, and subway subjects both at a local level as well as from around the province. Featured on the cover of a recent edition was a photo that instantly caught my eye. Taken by Neil McCarten, the Bloor and Bathurst intersection as it looked in 1966 brought back a flood of memories.

Having grown up just south of the intersection (758 Bathurst Street, third floor, phone Melrose 2154 — I'll always remember my first phone number) some of my earliest memories of the city took place in and around this corner. And even though the Filey family had moved to north Toronto by the time Neil snapped this photo, the image he captured was instantly recognizable to this Bathurst and Bloor kid.

Danforth Radio always had a window full of futuristic-looking radios and a store packed with the latest electrical appliances like irons, toasters, and washing machines. In fact, the name and status of Danforth Radio stayed with me long after and was probably why my wife and I bought our first colour TV (a Westinghouse console) from the Danforth Radio store in Yorkdale.

Just along the street was the Midtown Theatre. It began life as the Madison and is now called the Bloor. The Midtown was one of four movie houses in our neighbourhood, and while I called the Alhambra

Neil McCarten captured this view looking east on Bloor Street at Bathurst just days before the Feb. 26, 1966, opening of the Woodbine to Keele stretch of new Bloor-Danforth subway. The next day the streetcars were gone. Note the Danforth Radio and Midtown Theatre signs in both this photograph and the one on the next page..

Same view, today.

(north side of Bloor, west of Bathurst and long gone) "my" theatre, our gang would often cross Bathurst (with our parents' permission) to visit the Midtown. The other two theatres available to us were the Bloor (south side of Bloor, east of Bathurst, now a restaurant) and the Metro (south side of Bloor near Christie Pits), which is still a movie house, but now features films that are a far cry from the "Whip" Wilson and "Lash" LaRue westerns we used to watch.

While seeing the photo on the cover of that newsletter revived some happy memories, it also brought to mind a tragic event that occurred at that same corner on May 3, 1946.

I wasn't quite five years old when at about six o'clock p.m. a large machinery truck lost its brakes while descending the Bathurst hill north of Davenport Road. It hurtled down Bathurst Street, dodging traffic and pedestrians until it eventually slammed into a streetcar heading west on Bloor Street. Slicing into the truck's gas tank, PCC #4046 erupted in flames. Passengers scrambled to get off the burning car. Four died in the inferno, while fifty-three others were injured, one so severely that she passed away a few days later.

Anticipating my grandmother might have been on that streetcar, my mom and dad went to survey the scene. With no one to look after me,

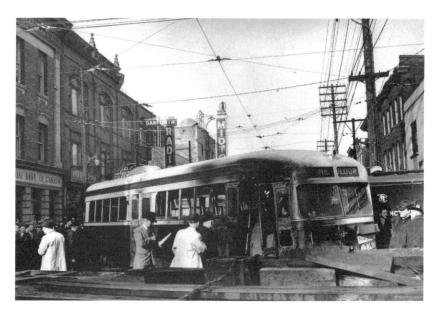

After being struck by a runaway truck on May 3, 1946, a badly damaged streetcar sits astride the Bathurst and Bloor intersection. Fifty-three passengers were injured, four fatally.

I naturally went with them. There's no doubt that seeing the aftermath of the collision imbedded fragments of that traumatic event into my childhood memory bank.

Things like the image of streetcar motorman, his head wrapped in towels, being assisted into a nearby store away from the flames, smoke, and noise. Or the smell of a burning awning like the ancient one on the Loblaws store at the southwest corner of the intersection. It had been sprayed with gasoline and was soon in flames. Even now, more than six decades later, I will occasionally smell the unmistakable odour of a smouldering tarpaulin somewhere and the memories of that sad early evening in May come rushing back.

August 24, 2008

Taking a Flight Back in Time

It was on August 31, 1938, that the first Canadian passenger plane, a Lockheed L-14 of the government-owned Trans-Canada Airlines (TCA, renamed Air Canada in 1965), landed at Toronto's new municipal airport. This airport was built by the Toronto Harbour Commission on farmland Toronto had acquired several miles northwest of the city near the quiet village of Malton, Ontario. The little community's name had been selected by its earliest settlers to honour their hometown in Yorkshire, England. Interestingly this site wasn't the only place the "experts" had looked at as the location for a new municipal airport. Other possibilities included a spot near Ashbridge's Bay, near the present-day Eglinton Avenue and

A Trans-Canada Airlines fourteen-seat Lockheed Super Electra similar to the one that holds the distinction of being the first Canadian airliner to land at Malton Airport.

This postcard view shows a TCA Super Constellation on the tarmac in front of Malton's one-storey terminal building. Erected in 1949, it served the flying public for the next fifteen years.

Laird Drive intersection in Leaside, north of the Dufferin Street and Wilson Avenue corner and at the western tip of Toronto Island. At first the "experts" felt the latter site was the best of them all, but soon changed their minds and gave the Malton location the nod.

Now, while the fourteen-passenger TCA aircraft may have been an early arrival it wasn't the first to touch down at the still unfinished airport. That distinction goes to a DC-3 of the privately-owned American Airlines (AA) that had landed at Malton two days earlier, August 29, 1938.

In a typical American entrepreneurial move, AA was eager to be the first foreign airline to obtain a franchise that would permit it to establish an international service between Toronto and various cities south of the border.

To show it was serious, the management of American Airlines organized a "goodwill flight." The trip originated in Chicago and stops were made along the way in Detroit and Buffalo where civic officials and media representatives from those cities boarded the craft. Joining the Buffalo contingent were Toronto controllers Conboy and Hamilton who had made their way to that city so they could join the crowd.

The local newspapers described the last leg of the flight recording that "the giant, streamlined DC-3 roared across Lake Ontario at 190 miles per hour." In the same story it was confirmed that "while the airline company had already made more than 25,000 flights over Canadian territory it had never until yesterday (August 29, 1938) been granted permission to land any of its aircraft at a Canadian airport."

Before the aircraft landed at Malton, where a crowd of three thousand awaited its arrival, Captain W.B. Whiteacre flew his plane over the CNE giving the thousands visiting the fair a chance to see (and hear) the giant silver monoplane that many regarded as "one of the wonders of the modern world."

On the other hand, the TCA flight that arrived two days after the historic AA flight took place without any pomp or ceremony. The Ottawa delegation on board was in town to simply talk about the still somewhat vague future of the new facility. In fact, the Minister of Transport, C.D. Howe, arrived at the meeting by train.

One last note, seventy years ago there was just the one flight into and out of the airport. Now there is an average of 1,200 arrivals and departures daily.

August 31, 2008

She's the Belle of Lake Ontario

On September 8, 1954, one of the most exciting stories in Canadian history began to take shape. And when that event concluded nearly twenty-one hours later, almost every Canadian (of which there were 15,287,000) was finally able to breathe a sigh of relief. The Toronto youngster had accomplished what no other person had done. Sixteen-year-old Marilyn Bell had conquered the cold, dark waters of Lake Ontario.

Since her conquest of the lake on September 8 and 9, 1954, many others have also completed the difficult crossing. However, none of those victories over Lake Ontario has created the drama and excitement that resulted from that very first attempt.

In retrospect, the entire event appears to have been based on a first-run movie script. (In fact, CBC did a made for TV movie titled *Heart* many years later.) To start, the swim itself was an attraction concocted by officials of the Canadian National Exhibition as a way to increase the number of people visiting the 1954 edition of the fair. And the heroine of the piece would, without any doubt, be the American marathon swimmer Florence Chadwick who had already conquered the English Channel, in both directions, and the 26 miles between the California coastline and Catalina Island.

So while Lake Ontario would be a challenge, for Florence it would be "a piece of cake." Her prize for completing the 32 mile swim from Youngstown, New York, to the breakwall south of the Exhibition Grounds — a whopping $10,000 (don't forget this was 1954 when the adult admission to the CNE was 50 cents, a return train ride to Montreal was $13, and a two-storey house in Leaside was $23,900).

Oh, and if by some bizarre chance Florence was unsuccessful the American swimmer would get nothing. (It was later announced that Florence had actually received $2,500 to cover her expenses.)

And speaking of nothing, the CNE officials announced that they would not recognize any other person who might have the audacity to attempt a similar swim during the period of the Exhibition. And even if they were to complete the crossing they would get nothing, period.

After a couple of false starts because of bad weather Florence entered the lake on the evening of September 8. Marilyn, recognizing there was nothing in it for her other than the chance to prove that a Canadian could do what the American was supposed to do, entered the lake shortly after Florence. They swam some distance apart, but stroke for stroke, and members of the media assigned to cover the swim began asking who this unknown competitor was.

Marilyn kept up the pace, and before long the sixteen-year-old Toronto-born schoolgirl's name was on everybody's lips, then in their notebooks, and soon on the airwaves.

Suddenly, at 5:45 in the morning of September 9, a nauseous Florence was taken from the water. The lake had defeated the American

From the Toronto Telegram, courtesy of the Toronto Sun *archives.*

Sixteen-year-old Toronto schoolgirl Marilyn Bell touches the breakwall south of the Palais Royale as she completes her momentous crossing of Lake Ontario, fifty-four years ago.

Marilyn Bell Dilascio, seen here with Mike Filey, arrives at the Toronto City Centre Airport prior the unveiling of a National Historic Sites and Monuments Board plaque.

Photo by Ken Lundy.

professional. But not the Canadian! Marilyn was still swimming and now all the attention was focused on her. As the only one of the trio that started out (Winnie Roach Leuszler, another Canadian who started the swim, had also been pulled from the water) the youngster soon became the sole topic of discussion, not just at the CNE waterfront, but across the city and within hours across the entire nation.

However, her victory was less than assured. In fact, there were occasions when it appeared the lake had defeated her, too. Finally, exactly 20 hours and 57 minutes after leaving the shoreline at Youngstown, Marilyn touched the breakwall, but not where the CNE officials had hoped. Winds and currents had altered her course, resulting in her actually completing a much longer crossing at the breakwall south of the Palais Royale. The accolades and gifts were not long in coming. Oh, and somewhat ashamedly, the CNE broke down and gave her not the amount promised the American, but a discounted $7,500.

Several weeks ago Marilyn, now Marilyn Bell Dilascio and living in New Jersey, arrived in Toronto on a Porter Airlines flight from Newark to attend the unveiling of a new National Historic Sites and Monuments

Board plaque. That plaque, which will be erected close to where she came ashore, describes her accomplishment fifty-four years ago as not just something of which Torontonians are proud of, but emphasizes that the event was of truly national significance.

Now if we can just get the people at the Order of Canada to finally recognize Marilyn not just for her many swimming accomplishments, but for her devotion to helping youngsters and the handicapped.

September 7, 2008

* The Toronto City Centre Airport was renamed the Billy Bishop Toronto City Airport in November 2009.

A Grave Story Indeed

Several years ago, while searching for a few final facts for a story that appeared in this column, I came across a fascinating story hidden in a collection of old newspaper clippings kept by the people in the *Toronto Sun*'s News Research Centre. Unfortunately there were no identifying marks on the ancient piece of newsprint, making the date the story was written and in what Toronto newspaper (of which there were at least five back then) appear virtually impossible to deduce. Oh, the title of the article that caught my eye? "The Murderers' Graveyard." It featured the story of an abandoned burial site behind the Don Jail on Gerrard Street East, and while I have no actual date, the article appeared to reference the hanging of one John Boyd, which makes it obvious that the story ran sometime after January 8, 1908.

Now fast forward about five years, and on September 2, 2008, the Cemeteries Regulation Unit of the Ontario Ministry of Small Business and Consumer Services placed a "Notice of Declaration" in a local newspaper. It reported that a burial site located at the Old Don Jail had recently been reported to the Registrar. It went on to request that "representatives" of the persons interred in the small graveyard behind the jail contact the Registrar.

I put two and two together and concluded that this was the same graveyard that was described in the story I found in the *Toronto Sun* archives.

What follows is that article word for word.

The Don Jail was subject of this early 1900s souvenir picture postcard.

The Murderers' Graveyard

Within the high walls which surround Toronto's jail is a little graveyard. Nowhere, perhaps, in Canada, is it possible to find a sadder spot. No memorial is erected, no flowers deck the graves, only a few mounds are there to mark the place in which repose the remains of those who shed the blood of their fellow-men and paid the penalty of their crime upon the gallows. (Note: The site was subsequently covered with asphalt.)

A new grave shows the resting place of Paul Steffoff who, for lust of gold, hacked a fellow countryman to pieces in a little house on Eastern avenue. Close by are laid the remains of Harry Williams, who shot and killed John Edward Varcoe while robbing the latter's store during the night of November 4th, 1899. On the wall above the grave are rudely cut, evidently by some prisoner, the initials H.W.

Over there lies Robert Coulter, who, in the presence of between two or three thousand people, expiated the crime of murdering James Kenny on the night of November 18, 1861. And there lies John Traviss, who died on the gallows confessing his guilt on November 23rd, 1871.

A present-day photo taken at the rear of the old Don Jail. The graves were located under the parking lot that was built on the site of a former exercise yard.

And there the remains of George Bennett, who on March 23, 1880, shot down Hon. George Brown [Note: Brown as the founder of the Globe newspaper] and who on the scaffold coolly said: "I am prepared to die. All I have to say is — May God have mercy on my soul."

And Robert Neil, who plunged a knife into the abdomen of John Rutledge, a guard at the Central Prison, when the latter entered the former's cell on the morning of January 13, 1888. Never did retribution follow so closely on a crime in Toronto, the murderer meeting his fate on February 10th, the same year. [Note: This hanging took place less than a month after the murder!]

There lie the perpetrators of murders of more recent date; Alexander Martin, who was found guilty of slaying his infant child by striking it with an oar of a boat off Munro Park and John Boyd, who died on the gallows on January 8th, 1908, for the shooting of Edward Wandel in a little room above a store on York street.

Then comes the grave of Steffoff, the last of the sad procession of those who have marched to the scaffold at the present jail building.

Frederick Lee Rice was the only murderer hanged at the jail who was not buried in the yard. Rice was a member of the gang which attempted to escape from the constables while being taken to jail in a hack after their trial for burglary committed in Aurora. Pistols were thrown into the cab by a third person, whose identity was never discovered. Rice shot Constable Boyd in the desperate struggle which ensued, and for this he was tried, convicted and hanged. His body was claimed by relatives in the United States, and was taken to that country for burial.

Though no longer a penal institution (it was closed as such in 1977), the Don Jail, or the Toronto Jail as it was officially designated, saw its first prisoners in 1864. Interestingly, though, official documents indicate the first hanging took place in what was referred to as the "new" jail (the previous one was on the north side of King Street just west of Church) on June 1, 1863. On that day Robert Coulter paid the price for murdering James Kenny. The hanging was a public spectacle, a trait that was abolished six years later. Over the following years thirty-three more felons were hanged at the Don. In fact, the jail has the distinction of "hosting" the last acts of capital punishment in the country when Ronald Turpin and Arthur Lucas were hanged on December 11, 1962.

The original Don Jail is now owned by the nearby Bridgepoint Health Centre. That institution is planning to "recycle" the historic structure for a variety of uses.

The building east of the old Don Jail was opened in 1958 and is still in use.

September 14, 2008

Stagnant Gardens

One of Toronto's best-known landmark buildings has been in the media recently, not for what is happening, but rather for what is *not* happening. Since its abandonment in 2001 following the move of the Maple Leafs hockey team to its new home in the Air Canada Centre in February 1999, and a number of games played over the following two years by the Toronto Rock lacrosse team, nothing much happened to the "house that Smythe built."

Then in 2004 things began looking up when it was announced that Loblaw Companies had purchased the building. What followed was talk of a large grocery and department store combination moving into the old building, and in doing so giving the place a new lease on life.

What followed were howls of derision from those who thought the very idea of a grocery/department store combo occupying the interior of the structure a diabolical proposal. "The grand old building should remain an arena and an arena with ice," many demanded. After all, it is a historic building.

The fact of the matter however is this: even though the building had been designated under the Ontario Heritage Act by city council back in 1990, that "protection" does not guarantee that the Gardens will stand forever. Its future remains in the hands of its owner, Loblaws. Incidentally, the same thing can be said for all the other designated buildings and not just those here in Toronto, but anywhere in the province. The provincial

This remarkable photo of Toronto's new Maple Leaf Gardens was taken on October 1, 1931, a mere forty-three days before the first Leafs played their first game in the new arena.

act that pertains to heritage structures is just not that strong. We all have to hope that Loblaws comes up with a plan that will result in the Gardens being revived, both physically and financially. No one else is going to do it.

While I'm on the subject of our beloved Gardens, it was on September 21, 1931, that its cornerstone was tapped into place by Lieutenant Governor W.R. Ross. Unlike most buildings that have their cornerstone installed at the start of construction (and traditionally at the northeast corner), Connie Smythe's new $1.5 million home for his Toronto Maple Leafs hockey team was well on its way to completion when the lieutenant governor did the deed (at the southeast corner).

Less than two months later, the Leafs team was on the ice playing the very first game in what had been dubbed "the house that Smythe built."

While the hometown team lost that first game to Chicago 2–1 in front of 15,542 spectators (the greatest number to ever watch a hockey game in Toronto history), Leafs fans take heart; our boys in blue and white went on to win that season's Stanley Cup.

September 21, 2008

This colourful Maple Leaf Gardens program highlighted the 1945 edition of the Ice Capades.

When Joy Came to Town

What do the following three things have in common: a Toronto discount gas station, a street in suburban Detroit, Michigan, and a gentleman who helped finance what would become one of the finest automobiles ever produced on this continent? Give up? Read on.

Often when the subject of why we're paying such high prices for gas comes up one of the reasons given is the lack of competition. Many will recall when the streets were lined with gasoline stations, the names of which are now only memories. Places like FINA, Gulf, Good Rich, Supertest, White Rose, B-A, Texaco, and Lion. In fact, I recall a time when you wouldn't fill up at the first station on the block because you

Art Chappelle created this fine painting of one of the city's several distinctive Joy gas stations.

knew the guy down the street would often be a few pennies a gallon cheaper. And when was the last time you took advantage of prices created by a gas "price war"? Over time most of the companies mentioned above either packed it in when they were unable to purchase product or were bought out usually by the big companies. As a result, there are now just four major brands available to the driving public. Fewer brands equals less competition, equals higher prices, or am I missing something?

One of the smaller gas stations I neglected to mention was Joy, a creation of Margaret Austin, the wife of a businessman and entrepreneur living in Detroit.

September 28, 2009

Goodbye Dominion, Hello Metro

Over the last number of years we've lost companies whose names were known to just about every Canadian. Remember these department stores, Woolworth's, Kresge's, Northway, Metropolitan, Morgan's, and the once-iconic Simpsons and Eatons? Or how about Aikenheads hardware, the ubiquitous United Cigar stores, the sweet-smelling Scanlans and Women's Bakery, and those little Downeyflake donut shops? Or appliance

This photo of a local Dominion store is dated 1939. The small street sign near the people waiting for a streetcar reads "Bathurst."

The Ontario Heritage Trust recently unveiled a commemorative plaque at the Stevenson Farm near Alliston. It was here that grocery store founder Theodore Loblaw spent his childhood years. Present at the unveiling were Loblaws' representative Inge van den Berg, and Stephen Milne, who operates a bed and breakfast in the historic Stevenson farmhouse (stevensonfarms.com).

stores like Danforth Radio and Eddie Black? And just around almost every corner one could find a Carload, Superior, Stop and Shop, or William Davies grocery store. All of these names are now just part of our history.

And speaking of grocery stores, even as I write this column two more familiar names in that business are in the process of being removed from the streetscape, as both the Dominion and A&P titles are replaced by name of their new owner, Metro.

While A&P (originally The Great Atlantic and Pacific Tea Company) is the older of these two stores with a founding date south of the border of 1859, of more interest north of that same border is the demise of the Dominion store name, a title that identifies a company that came into being here in Canada on October 3, 1919.

The concept of what would become Dominion Stores was actually born a year earlier on a golf course in New Hampshire when a visiting Canadian commented to his host businessman Robert Jackson that Americans must really love tea, there being such a proliferation of Atlantic & Pacific Tea Company stores in the cities and towns he had visited while on vacation. Surprised that there were no similar stores north of the border Jackson decided to investigate, and after a brief visit to Toronto returned home convinced that a chain of grocery stores operating in a fashion similar to the way the American A&P did (that is selling items such as sugar, flour, soap in bulk) would be successful in Ontario's capital city.

He was also able to convince his friend William Pentland, at the time manager of all the A&P stores throughout Connecticut, to join him in the venture. Together they opened two stores in Toronto, one at 174 Wallace Avenue and the other at 779 Queen Street East. Their enterprise, which was named in honour of the country in which Jackson and Pentland had set up shop (back then it was still called the Dominion of Canada), was a success from the start. In fact, it wasn't long before the two men purchased and renamed an additional eighteen stores scattered across the city and operated by a competitor. And the name of that competitor? T.P. Loblaw.

That wasn't the only time the Dominion and Loblaws businesses were to cross paths. In September of 1929 officials of the two companies announced that a deal that would see Dominion purchase the entire Loblaws chain of stores was in the works. Less than two months later the merger was called off, citing the "present financial conditions" (also known as the Great Depression) as the prime reason.

The two companies continued on their separate ways here in Toronto with Dominion eventually being acquired by the Argus Corporation and then by A&P Canada. All Dominion and A&P stores are in the process of being folded into the Metro Inc. basket.

In 1947 George Weston Ltd. began purchasing stock in Loblaws, and by the early 1950s had gained controlling interest.

Recently the founder of Loblaws, Theodore Pringle Loblaw, was recognized with an Ontario Heritage Trust plaque erected at his childhood home just outside Alliston, Ontario.

October 5, 2008

New, Old Electric Railway

Over the past few weeks we have been inundated with a whole host of announcements trumpeting a project that if and when implemented will make it easier for us to get around the sprawling Greater Toronto Area. Now all somebody has to do is find the billions and billions of dollars necessary to get things rolling.

While the public transit component of this massive project sounds revolutionary, in many respects it's not far off from the idea of a commuter service proposed nearly a century ago by Sir Adam Beck, the father of Ontario Hydro. Beck's proposal, which he first put forward in 1912, was to build a network of high-speed electric railways that would operate along hydro transmission line corridors and use power generated by the company. They were dubbed "radial" railways because they would radiate out from major Ontario cities and connect with nearby municipalities.

Locally, the plan was to connect the provincial capital with Uxbridge, Newmarket, Markham, and Port Perry. Another line would run from Toronto to London via Port Credit and Guelph, while a third would see radial cars operating to and from Toronto all the way to Niagara Falls and Fort Erie via St Catharines.

The outbreak of the Great War in 1914 combined with the fact that a number of communities didn't want a radial line running through their jurisdiction. Then there came a change in provincial governments, with the new regime under E.C. Drury dead set against his arch rival's radial

Bond Lake Park, located just east of Yonge Street south of Aurora, was a favourite amusement spot for Torontonians. In this view taken on June 20, 1924, a group of Toronto & York Radial Railway cars delivers families to the park for their church's annual picnic.

plan. These stumbling blocks plus the miles of new highways that were built after the war's end and the proliferation of new automobiles that were now available to just about anyone proved to be too much. By 1922 the revolutionary Beck radials scheme was dead.

That's not to say that the concept of high speed electric streetcars was never implemented in the Toronto area. In fact, there were several privately owned radial lines that connected outlying communities with the big city. Using specially modified streetcars these lines served Woodbridge, Guelph, and Port Credit, as well as West Hill east of the city.

But of all the Toronto radials the most successful line and the one that stayed in business the longest was the "Metropolitan." Incorporated as a horse-car line in 1877, it operated on Yonge Street from a point near the beautifully restored LCBO store (near today's Summerhill subway station) to terminals that were moved further and further north as business warranted.

This line was electrified in 1889 (three years before the city streetcars) and one year later the end of the line was moved to York Mills. Extensions to Richmond Hill, then even further north to Newmarket opened in 1896 and 1899, respectively. Six years later the high-speed cars were operating over a private right-of-way into the community of Jackson's Point on Lake Simcoe. In 1909 the big green Metropolitan radial cars rolled into Sutton.

This 1948 photo by Bill Hood shows North Yonge Railways radial car #416 resting at the Glen Echo loop at the city limits on Yonge Street. The market in the background is now the site of a Loblaw's store. The last radial car rumbled into history sixty years ago.

Traffic on the radial cars was especially high during the summer months. Incidentally, a portion of the Metropolitan right-of-way along the south shore of the lake is now called Metro Road.

Increasing highway traffic eventually resulted in decreasing ridership and on March 16, 1930, the Metropolitan line was abandoned. However, it wasn't long before pressure from the communities between Toronto and Richmond Hill to continue some form of radial service resulted in the line being reopened as far north as the latter community.

However, power shortages that had been plaguing the province ever since the end of the Second World War convinced the line's new operator, the TTC, to convert the last remnant of the once ubiquitous electric radials to diesel bus operation. The last full day of radial car service was on October 9, 1948. On the same day the TTC's Spadina streetcar line was also converted to bus operation.

The question now is will Yonge Street see streetcars (in the form of "light rail vehicles") when the multi-billion dollar transit master plan is implemented? Stranger things have happened. After all, streetcars replaced buses on the Spadina route in 1997.

October 12, 2008

Landmark of Learning

One of the best known of our dwindling Toronto landmark buildings is the former Knox Theological College located in the centre of Spadina Avenue just north of College Street. The building's official address is 1 Spadina Crescent.

Prior to the Presbyterian Church selecting this privately owned site — known back then as Crescent Garden — for its new college (to replace its prior facility on Grosvenor Street), the city fathers had considered buying the property from the Baldwin Estate and turning it into a small park. When that plan fell through the land was sold to the church for $10,000.

The Toronto architectural firm of Smith and Gemmel was then selected to design the new school, and on August 27, 1873, the architects placed an advertisement in the *Globe* soliciting parties interested in erecting the new building at a cost not to exceed $120,000.

With the preliminary details worked out on April 2, 1874, the cornerstone of what was to be known as Knox College was tapped into place by one of the founders of the city's original Knox Presbyterian Church, the Honourable John McMurrich. Just sixteen months later, October 6, 1875, to be precise, the new building was officially opened.

The building continued as a Presbyterian College for the next thirty-nine years before classes were moved in 1914 to its new St. George Street location on the University of Toronto campus. To accommodate the hundreds of wounded returning from the battlefields in Europe the

Spadina Avenue looking north to Knox Theological College from College Street, circa 1890. Note the horse-drawn streetcar making its way around the building bound for the route's northern terminal at Bloor. In addition, a man can be seen to the left of centre pushing the newest sensation of the age, a bicycle, across the street.

old college was converted into a military hospital. One of the nursing aides that worked for a time in this medical facility was Amelia Earhart, who, while visiting a sister attending school in Toronto and seeing the wounded and maimed young men, decided to stay in town to help in any way she could.

After the war the old college became a veterans' hospital, and so it remained until 1943 when it was purchased by Connaught Laboratories. It was here that a variety of pharmaceutical products were developed, manufactured, and tested.

In 1972 the University of Toronto purchased the now ancient (by Toronto standards) building, and today it is home to the U of T's Ophthalmology Department's Eyebank of Canada.

An interesting adjunct to the history of this old building came to light while I was researching this story. In a 1908 edition of a local newspaper it was reported that the Knox College building would soon be demolished and replaced by a twelve-storey building costing $1.25 million. It would be home to the Toronto branch of the British-Canadian Department

A similar view today.

Stores. The lower three floors of the building would be clad in granite and marble while the upper floors would be glazed in terracotta. Nothing further happened.

Two decades later another plan was put forward. This time the former college would be demolished and in its place a replacement for the Toronto Maple Leaf hockey team's old Mutual Street Arena would be built. Again nothing happened. Good!

November 2, 2008

Lest We Forget

On November 11 we will honour those who made the supreme sacrifice during two world wars, in Korea, and in Afghanistan — sacrifices that help ensure the freedoms that many of us take for granted.

One of the unavoidable consequences of war is the tremendous sums of money that must be raised to purchase the necessities to ensure victory. To that end, events known as Victory Loan Parades were introduced during the Great War in an effort to encourage the public to buy Victory Bonds.

During that conflict (one that many believed would actually be the "war to end all wars") there were several Victory Loan Parades through the streets of Toronto. To drum up extra interest, and hopefully extra sales of Victory Bonds, the parade held on November 21, 1917, featured the latest in warfare technology, the tank.

Introduced in the fall of the previous year during the Battle of the Somme, this new piece of fighting equipment, while not a total success, the tank (so called because the components of the earliest experimental models had been shipped in wooden containers that had contained water tanks and were still identified as such) threw a mighty scare into the minds and hearts of the enemy.

One of those British tanks, nicknamed "Britannia," was shipped to Canada where it was scheduled to appear in several Victory Loan parades. Here in Toronto a little extra was added when "Britannia" trundled down University Avenue and then, to demonstrate its power, up and over an old

Courtesy of the City of Toronto Archives.

A new tool of war, the tank, was a highlight in the city's Victory Loan Parade held on November 21, 1917. Here it is seen crushing an automobile in front of the old University Avenue Armouries. The car was empty at the time.

car that had been positioned in the middle of the road just in front of the Armouries, a building that was located on the east side of the avenue just north of Queen Street (and, incidentally, the reason why the small side street nearby is still called, albeit in the singular, Armoury Street). It was in this building that thousands joined up during the South African War, the two world wars, and the Korean conflict.

The Armouries was demolished in 1963, in spite of great protesting, and the present Court House erected on the site.

Oh, did that tank help raise additional money in that particular Victory Bond drive. Prior to the parade the city had raised $27 million, $3 million short of its objective. Less than two weeks later Torontonians had gone over the top, many suggested, thanks to the tank.

Buy a poppy, say a prayer.

November 9, 2008

Toronto in Transition

Up until September 1, 1921, the day on which Toronto's public transportation needs were turned over to the newly created and municipally operated Toronto Transportation Commission (the term Transportation became Transit with the opening of the Yonge subway in March, 1954), getting people around the growing city had been a task awarded to a privately owned concern called the Toronto Railway Company (TRC).

The TRC, under the direction of Sir William Mackenzie, one of the country's most powerful businessmen, had been granted this franchise in 1891. Mackenzie would hold the reins (figuratively speaking, that is, since the horses that pulled the little city streetcars had all been retired by 1894) for the next thirty years. Over those three decades Mackenzie's electric streetcar empire (which included public transit systems outside the city limits as well) made him a millionaire many times over.

However, his interest in making money for himself and the company shareholders soon compromised the company's day-to-day operations. Insufficient streetcars to handle the growing numbers of transit users combined with his refusal to extend streetcar lines into the growing suburban areas forced the city's hand. There would be no renewal of Mackenzie's franchise that placed a stranglehold on the city's streetcar service. The TRC's last full day of operations would be August 31, 1921. The very next day, September 1, 1921, the new TTC was in charge.

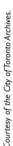

Children play a game of shinny hockey in front of the Toronto Civic Railway's Wychwood car house, 1915. The date over the carhouse door, 1913, is the year the original St. Clair streetcar route began.

In addition to Mackenzie's city streetcar lines, the TTC also took over the Toronto Civic Railways, a five route streetcar operation created by the city itself in 1911 to help alleviate the problem of getting people to and from the suburban areas that Mackenzie's company refused to service.

One of those Civic lines operated on St. Clair from Yonge westerly to the present Caledonia Road. In addition to the streetcars that ran on this route, the TTC also acquired a small carhouse on Bracondale (later Wychwood) Avenue. Opened in April 1914, it was here that the cars were serviced and stored when not in use. The carhouse was enlarged in 1916 and enlarged again following the takeover of the Civic Railways by the new TTC in 1921.

A children's playground is part of the new Artscape Wychwood Barns project that has brought new life to this heritage site located near St. Clair and Bathurst.

Over the following years Wychwood carhouse was a very busy place. Then in 1978 the property was declared surplus by the TTC and eventually abandoned.

But the Wychwood carhouse story isn't over. It's now the home of Artscape Wychwood Barns, a clever redevelopment and reuse of one of the city's few remaining heritage sites.

November 16, 2008

A Toronto Kingpin

Tommy Ryan was born in Guelph, Ontario, in 1872. While still a young man he decided to seek his fame and fortune in the big City of Toronto in 1890. Passing up a chance to sign a major league baseball contract Tommy decided instead to take on the responsibility of managing one of the city's largest billiard academies, located on the second floor of the Ryrie Building at 11 Temperance Street right in the heart of the city's business district.

In 1905 Tommy decided to supplement the hall's many billiard tables with a few wooden alleys, thereby introducing Canadians to the game of "regulation" ten-pin bowling, a game that had become extremely popular south of the border.

However, it quickly became obvious to Tommy that this new ten-pin bowling was far too strenuous for many of the more portly businessmen who stopped by for a game to while away the noon hour. More important, however, was the fact that the new game was far too time consuming. As a result many of his customers were forced to cut back on the length of time they would spend in the billiard hall's restaurant. That just wouldn't do.

But Tommy had a plan.

He arranged to have his father take five of the large pins to his woodworking shop where he whittled them down to about half their original size. Next Tommy had a local company manufacture a new type of bowling ball that was about half the size and weight of the ten-pin ball.

Right: Toronto's own Tommy Ryan, the inventor of five-pin bowling.

Below: A group of nattily attired gentlemen enjoy a game of ten-pin bowling at one of the city's nine early twentieth-century alleys. The crowd of spectators attests to the game's popularity.

And to keep those lighter pins from flying off in all directions when hit by the ball Tommy fitted out each one with a large band of gutta percha rubber specially made for Tommy by the Dominion Rubber Company located just down Yonge Street at the southeast corner of Front. Tommy revised the scoring system and called his new game five-pin bowling. The year was 1909.

Tommy Ryan never bothered to patent his idea or the equipment used to play the game. He was far too busy with other endeavours. He ran a hotel, loved horse racing, and was a successful boxing promoter, but most of all Tommy loved art and antiques. He opened an art gallery at 11 Grosvenor Street, and in the late 1920s moved into the former Massey mansion at 515 Jarvis Street (now the site of the Mansion Keg restaurant).

It was here that Tommy Ryan passed away on November 19, 1961, age 89.

By the way, while researching this column I came across a fascinating video clip on the internet. It's the *Tabloid* television show dated January 25, 1957. After the weather report by iconic weatherman Percy Saltzman, the show's hostess Joyce Davidson interviews the creator of five-pin bowling Tommy Ryan. Check it out at: *archives.cbc.ca/lifestyle/pastimes/clips/15874/.*

November 23, 2008

Tracking the Past

There's been a lot of talk in recent months about something called Transit City, an ambitious plan put forward by the City of Toronto and the TTC that when fully implemented would see seven new light rail transit lines serving passengers on the city's busiest transit routes. Providing service on these lines will be new, state-of-the art, fully accessible light rail vehicles operating on dedicated rights-of-way.

As ambitious as the Transit City plan may seem to today's Torontonians, there have been numerous other transit plans put forward over the decades, some of which were completed (i.e. the provision for a future "tube" [subway] beneath the roadway of the Prince Edward Viaduct), while others never quite made it off the drawing board (i.e. the early 1970s Krauss-Maffei magnetic levitation project at the CNE grounds).

One of the more interesting projects that did get built and did go into operation was one put forward in 1889 by the Belt Land Corporation, a syndicate of city business tycoons that included lawyer John Hoskin (Hoskin Avenue) and John Moore (Moore Avenue and Moore Park). The idea was to have the corporation acquire large tracts of vacant land north of the Second Concession (Bloor Street) then sell individual parcels on which eager homebuyers would erect new residences in the "highlands" far from the hustle and bustle of the busy city to the south. The promoters as well as the buyers were sure that in time real neighbourhoods would be created.

This view, from the Belt Land Corporation's promotional brochure, looks north on Yonge Street as one of the Belt Line steam trains crosses the bridge that is the most visible remnant of this pioneer version of GO Transit.

One concern people had about moving to the Belt Land properties was the remoteness of the site. To help alleviate this problem the corporation constructed two commuter railway lines over which steam-powered passenger trains would transport passengers from their suburban residences to the city's old Union Station at the foot of today's University Avenue, then home again at the end of the day.

There were two loops over which the Belt Line trains operated. To the west was the Humber Loop, which carried its passengers to Swansea, then northward to Lambton, east to the Junction area, then back to Union Station through Parkdale via the Grand Trunk tracks.

The other, known as the Don Loop, operated from Union Station east across the waterfront, north up the Don Valley to curve west just north of St. Clair, through Mount Pleasant Cemetery, crossing over Yonge Street via a substantial steel bridge, continuing west just north of Eglinton Avenue to the Grand Trunk railway corridor west of Caledonia, then south and back to Union Station.

Unfortunately, the building boom burst, and with properties failing to sell in sufficient numbers to keep the company "on track" the Belt Land Corporation folded in early 1892. However, since the tracks had

A similar view today. Kay Gardner was a local politician who championed the creation of the Belt Line trail.

already been laid the Grand Trunk railway decided to operate trains to serve those who had already moved into their new homes. That service continued until it became obvious that the total of all the 25 cent fares collected wouldn't be sufficient to pay the bills. On November 17, 1894, less than twenty-eight months after service began, this pioneer version of today's GO Transit was finally "derailed."

During the Great War the tracks on the eastern part of the Don Loop were torn up, melted down, and cast into tools of war. For many years the rest of the loop plus all of the Humber Loop continued to be used by freight trains until the city acquired the right-of-way and turned 2.8 miles of it into a recreational walking trail.

November 30, 2008

Bag to the Future

All the recent rhetoric at Toronto City Hall about reducing the number of plastic bags being hauled to area landfill sites brought back memories of a couple of part time jobs I had during my early years at North Toronto Collegiate. One job was bagging and delivering groceries on my bike for Mr. Valiquette's tiny Carload Groceteria store at the northeast corner of Mt. Pleasant and Erskine. The other was a short stint bagging items at the checkout counter at Sunnybrook Plaza's Power grocery store located in the second "shopping centre" built anywhere in the country. This historic plaza was, and still is, at the Bayview and Eglinton intersection. As I recall, my Power store looked not unlike the one in the photograph accompanying this article. How 'bout those bow ties?

Back when I was bagging groceries the plastic bag had either not been invented or, if it had, there weren't enough of them to cause a problem. We used paper bags and I know that millions of trees gave their lives so we could have had those paper bags, but trees are a renewable resource. Plastic bags, on the other hand, are made from petroleum (and other non-renewable things) via a rather circuitous process.

The paper bags we used were (and are still) called Kraft bags (the word Kraft means strength or power in German), were brown in colour, were strong, and you could fill each one with lots of stuff. Oh, and one other thing made them special. They were stacked in a flat pile on the counter and with a simple flick of the wrist the bag would snap wide open, wide

Check-out clerks wait to fill paper grocery bags at a Power store, 1953.

enough, in fact, to be able to fill it up with meat (wrapped in more brown paper), all sorts of groceries, tin cans, etcetera etcetera. They were called "snap-action" paper bags.

Now, I don't know whether the next part of my story is true or not. Someone once told me these environmentally-friendly "snap-action" paper bags were actually invented in the Kilgour Brothers factory of wealthy Toronto businessman Joseph Kilgour who lived at Sunnybrook Farm, a magnificent estate located a few miles north of the city.

Following his death in 1925 Alice, his widow, gave the land to the city for a park. And it was on a section of Sunnybrook Park that today's Sunnybrook Hospital (initially a military hospital) was built and opened in 1948.

December 7, 2008

Oh, How We've Grown

Every so often I'm asked "what's the population of Toronto?" Well, according to the city's own website it's 2.48 million. However, that figure is sometimes confused with the population of the GTA (Greater Toronto Area). That figure is 5.5 million, which is made up of the populations of the City of Toronto plus the neighbouring Regional Municipalities of York, Halton, Peel, and Durham.

Now that we've got those figures out of the way, go ahead and ask me "what was the population of Toronto in the year that it became a city?" That's easy. In 1834, the year that King William IV affixed his signature to an act titled "4th Wm. IV. Chapter 23" by which the Town of York was elevated to city status and given back its original name, exactly 9,254 people called Toronto home.

Over the years Toronto's population continued to increase. In fact, by 1901 the total number of Torontonians was 205,857. That number had been reached as a result of the annexation of a number of autonomous communities that surrounded the city. Citizens of Yorkville, Brockton, Seaton Village, Rathnally, Sunnyside, and Parkdale all became Torontonians before the nineteenth century ended.

Many more were added in the first decade of the next century when places such as Rosedale, Deer Park, East Toronto, Wychwood, Bracondale, West Toronto, Midway and Balmy Beach, Earlscourt, and Dovercourt were annexed. By 1911, the number of Torontonians had

The corner of Yonge and Eglinton, 1917, just five years after the Town of North Toronto became part of the big city to the south.

increased to exactly 374,667.

One of the largest increases occurred exactly ninety-six years ago tomorrow when on December 15, 1912, the Town of North Toronto became part of the big city to the south. But this annexation, which inflated the population figure to 410,036, didn't go quite as smoothly as the previous ones.

The citizens of North Toronto questioned how long it would be once they joined the city before they'd get a single-fare ride to and from the city. Up until now a second fare had to be paid in order to get north of the city limits, then located well south of St. Clair Avenue. Actually, it would take years before the TTC would service the community, a fact that almost led to the former town seceding from the union.

Meanwhile city officials were worried about the debt they would be saddled with since the town had recently borrowed heavily to improve the local water and sewer systems. In addition, the town's property assessment figures were somewhat suspect. Sound familiar?

The concerns over whether annexation would ultimately be good or bad were obvious in the speeches given at the dinner held on the night before the town was officially declared extinct.

In his comments, Councillor Baker of North Toronto declared "We are now partaking of a wedding banquet with the City of Toronto as the groom and the Town of North Toronto, being the weaker party, the

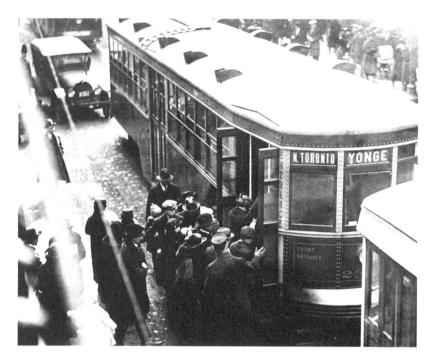

On a cold February day in 1922, passengers squeeze on board one of the TTC's new Peter Witt streetcars at a stop on Yonge just north of Queen. While the car's destination sign reads "N. Toronto," the end of the line was still well south of St. Clair Avenue.

bride. As in all such cases, the bride is being committed to the tender mercies of the groom."

History tells us this "marriage" turned out just fine.

December 14, 2008

*The Greater Toronto Area (the City of Toronto plus the Regional Municipalities of Durham, Peel, Halton, and York) has a population of 5.5 million as of August 2010.

A Surprise Demolition

Work on the restoration of Toronto's historic St. Lawrence Hall at the southwest corner of the King and Jarvis intersection was actually a little ahead of schedule that Friday afternoon in March 1967. Unfortunately, that good news wouldn't last.

The restoration of the old building that had been constructed in 1850-51 as the city's new social centre had actually been proposed in

TO BUILDERS.

SEALED TENDERS will be received at this Office until noon on MONDAY, the 27th inst. [after which no Tender will be received] from persons desirous of Contracting for the whole of the works to be performed in the Erection of the

CENTRE OF THE

NEW BLOCK OF BUILDINGS,

King Street, on the site of the Old City Hall.

The Drawings and Specifications may be seen, and all other neceseary information obtained, at the Office of Wм. Thomas, Esq., Architect, Church Street, any day after Tuesday, the 21st instant, during office hours.

The Lowest Tender will not be accepted, unless otherwise satisfactory.

Securities will be required for the due performance of the Contract.

By order,

CHARLES DALY,
C. C. C.

CLERK'S OFFICE,
Toronto, August 16, 1849.   439-td

This ad appeared in the *Globe* newspaper on August 16, 1849.

117

This early 1900s postcard view shows the St. Lawrence Hall and to the right of the view the old north market and the now-demolished overhead walkway that connected it with the south market on Front Street.

1962 as one part of a major redevelopment plan for the area bounded by King, Jarvis, Front, and Scott Streets. Included in this plan would be a 1,500-seat theatre, a small concert hall, a repertory house, an art gallery containing several lecture halls, and an office tower just across east of the two-year-old O'Keefe (now Sony) Centre. All these new buildings, plus the restored St. Lawrence Hall, would be known collectively as the St. Lawrence Cultural Centre and would be the city's way of honouring the centennial of Canadian confederation.

For a variety of reasons, both financial and political (sound familiar?), the entire project was soon in trouble. Eventually all the new buildings in the project were put on hold. However, thanks to the determination of the Toronto Chapter of the Ontario Association of Architects and members the Toronto Construction Association, along with vast encouragement from the well-respected heritage advocate Professor Eric Arthur, it was agreed by all concerned that the restoration of the St. Lawrence Hall would proceed.

In early August 1966, Toronto City Council authorized work to start. Because it was in the worst condition structurally, restoration of the west side of the building was undertaken first. Work continued through the fall and winter months. Then, as the restoration of the east (Jarvis Street) side

Late in the afternoon of March 10, 1967, the east wing of Toronto's "ancient" St. Lawrence Hall collapsed into the Jarvis and King intersection. Restoration of this historic building was in real jeopardy.

of the old building was underway ... trouble! It was late in the afternoon of Friday, March 10, 1967, when the job foreman noticed that small pieces of mortar were falling from the interior walls. The building seemed to give itself a slight shake. It was obvious something was wrong. He quickly had the structure evacuated, telling some of his men to clear the intersection of people and vehicles. Within seconds the entire east wing of the ancient structure collapsed in a huge pile of bricks, mortar, and splintered wood. Fortunately, the warnings had prevented any loss of life or major damage other than that suffered by the building itself.

As bad as it looked, officials were sure the setback could be overcome, but timing was critical if the project was to be completed by year's end so it could be identified as a true Centennial of Canadian Confederation project.

And made it they did, when on December 28, 1967, Governor General Rolly Michener did the honours when he declared the restored St. Lawrence Hall back in business.

An interesting aside, the anticipated financial assistance from the Ontario government was withheld as the province had its own centennial project in mind, the Ontario Science Centre. It missed being a true Centennial Year project since our Science Centre didn't open until the fall of 1969. That was one year before another component of the city's original Centennial Year venture, a project now known as the St. Lawrence Centre for the Performing Arts, finally opened to the public.

December 28, 2008

Birth of Sunday Sports

Headlines in the sports section of the three Toronto daily newspapers on January 4, 1950, might just as well have read "Play Ball!" Now, you may wonder why such a statement would be made on a cold winter's day in Toronto. Actually those two words made perfect sense if one was to inspect the results of the municipal election that had been held just two days earlier.

On January 2, 1950, (back then municipal elections were held on the first day of January) in addition to electing long-time city politician Hiram McCallum to another term as Toronto's mayor, the electorate had defied all the opinion polls and by a majority of 6,315 agreed to ask the provincial government (after all, the city was, and still is a "child" of the province) to allow Sunday sports within the city limits.

For the record here are the actual words of that historic plebiscite: "Are you in favour of the City of Toronto seeking legislation to make amateur, professional and other forms of commercial sport legal on Sunday?"

While "Buck" McCallum's return to City Hall as Chief Magistrate was pretty much a foregone conclusion (he had served in that capacity since 1948), the fact that 88,108 citizens had agreed that it was time to permit sporting events on Sunday came as a total shock. In fact, in one pre-election poll that was conducted amongst all the candidates seeking office in the 1950 election a total of thirty-five voiced their opposition to the idea. Only six agreed that it was time to put aside the Lord's Day Act

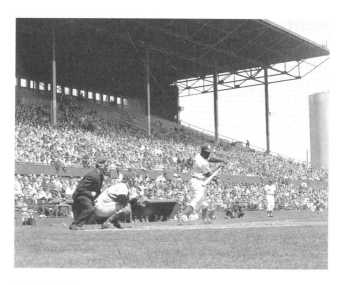

Maple Leaf Stadium, pictured here in the early 1950s, was located on the southwest corner of Lakeshore Boulevard and Bathurst Street. Toronto's very first professional sporting event was held at the stadium on May 7, 1950. Toronto lost.

(legislation that had been on the books for decades) and allow the playing of sports on Sunday. In addition, 1,100 members of the Citizen's Committee Opposing Sunday Sport went door-to-door urging those who could vote to reject the idea.

The rejection of the idea seemed like a slam dunk. However, to the amazement of virtually all Torontonians, the idea of seeking approval from the province to allow Sunday sports won the day. That approval was subsequently given, with the first Sunday baseball game held on May 7, 1950, when the Toronto Maple Leafs of the International League played a double-header against the New Jersey Giants. Our guys lost the first game 9–5. And just when it looked as if we'd lose the second 4–1, fate stepped in. One requirement of all those early Sunday games was that they had to be over by 5:59 p.m. Anticipating a loss, the Toronto players slowed things down by dropping the ball between pitches, calling time-outs, and so on. When the 5:59 p.m. curfew kicked in, only five innings had been played. The game was called a "no decision" and replayed the following June. The team still lost.

Incidentally, one city politician who supported the Sunday sports concept from the start was Allan Lamport. He literally put his job at City Hall on the line. Not only was his belief that Toronto was ready for a more

Maple Leaf Stadium was a popular place, especially on Sundays once the province gave the "OK" to playing professional sports on the Sabbath.

"open" Sunday vindicated, in that same election Lamport was elected to the powerful Board of Control and two years later he was elected mayor. By the way, this is the same Allan Lamport who suggested nearly a half-century ago that the Cross-Waterfront Expressway (later renamed the Gardiner) be built as a toll road so there'd be funds available in the future to maintain it.

January 4, 2009

Historic Snow Days

It happens every winter here in this part of the world. It gets dark early, the bottom falls out of the thermometer, and we get ... wait for it ... snow. And, as annoying as these events may be, for most of us (what, some actually enjoy these facts of winter life?) none of them are unexpected. The photos that accompany this column were selected to prove that the winter of 2008-09 is really no different than the winters of years past.

Oh, and while we're on the subject of snow, everyone knows that cats must be smarter than dogs. There's no way you could get eight of them to pull a sled though snow.

January 11, 2009

Here we see one of the privately owned radial streetcars (called radials because they radiated out from the city) navigating huge snow drifts on Yonge Street in the suburban hinterland somewhere north of the city, perhaps between Thornhill and Richmond Hill. Beginning in the early 1900s these big green cars ran from the Toronto city limits, then south of St. Clair Avenue, as far north as Lake Simcoe. Now they're discussing constructing an electric line (subway or light rail) that will once again connect the city with its northern neighbours.

Boy, they could use one of these snow removal machines on our side street here in North York. Back in 1937 when this photo was taken on Bay Street just north of Queen's Quay, instead of moving the snow from Point A to Point B and then back to Point A, crews actually removed the snow altogether much to the fascination of crowds of onlookers. Note the eight-year-old Royal York Hotel in the background.

Still the reigning champion of twenty-four-hour snowfalls here in Toronto is the one that occurred on December 12–13, 1944. Over that period of time more than 20 inches of snow fell on a city that was expecting "a few flurries." This view looks north on Yonge Street from Gerrard Street a few hours after the storm passed. Some traffic was moving, including a bread truck and the omnipresent Peter Witt motor and trailer streetcars on Yonge.

Bridging the Gap

It was on January 16, 1915, that work officially began on what at the time was known simply as the Bloor Street Viaduct. Today we know that nearly one-mile long structure as either the Bloor-Danforth Viaduct or the Prince Edward Viaduct, the latter title bestowed on the bridge by city council on September 11, 1919. While the prince hadn't actually cut a ribbon or unveiled a commemorative plaque, Edward had been driven

Toronto Mayor Tommy Church watches as dignitaries take part in the sod turning for the Don Section of the new Bloor-Danforth Viaduct on January 16, 1915.

This progress photo was taken by city photographer Arthur Goss on February 22, 1917, and shows the state of construction of the westernmost piers of the new viaduct. When taking this photo Mr. Goss and his camera were positioned on the right-of-way of the future Don Valley Parkway.

across the viaduct in Sir John Eaton's Rolls Royce during the prince's brief visit to the city earlier in the year.

By the way I started this article by stating that this extraordinary project "officially began" nintey-four years ago because many months of preliminary design work had already been undertaken prior to Toronto Mayor Tommy Church removing that first chunk of frozen sod from the floor of the Don Valley on January 16, 1915. But the viaduct idea is much, much older than that.

Present at the brief ceremony was a crowd of about two hundred people. Among them were several elected officials, a couple of senior city officials, and a Mr. Black who was the project engineer and attended the ceremony as the representative of the Montreal-based contractors, Quinlan and Robertson.

Not present in that crowd, for reasons that weren't explained in any of that day's newspaper reports, were several people who were closely connected with the $2.5 million plan to connect the city with the area on the east side of the Don Valley.

Among them was Roland Caldwell Harris, the city's Public Works

Commissioner and the person who was ultimately responsible for the completion of the project that was achieved both on budget and on schedule.

Another was Thomas Taylor, who was Chief of the Bridge Section of the city's Works Department. Taylor would enter the city's history books as the designer of the viaduct.

The third "no-show" was William Maclean. "Billy" Maclean was born in Hamilton but spent most of his working career in the newspaper business here in Toronto. In fact, he even started his own newspaper, the *World*, in 1880. In it he constantly promoted the idea of constructing a massive bridge that would connect a sandy trail called Danforth Avenue east of the Don Valley with one of the city's major east-west thoroughfares west of the valley, Bloor Street.

Without that connection Maclean argued that east Toronto would never grow and prosper. He also criticized the city for spending too much time and money on the western part of the city while ignoring areas east of the Don River.

Maclean seemed to be a voice in the wilderness. The city did put the idea of building a viaduct across the Don Valley on the municipal ballot on three separate occasions (1910, 1911, and 1912), and with estimates increasing from $750,000 to $1.8 million it seemed the time just wasn't right. But Billy persisted.

Then on the fourth attempt, which was presented to the Toronto voters on January 1, 1913, by a majority of 9,236, the proposal to erect a high-level viaduct across the Don Valley was approved. This time the anticipated cost of the project had more than tripled over original estimates.

Billy Maclean died on December 7, 1929. Some death notices suggested that the Prince Edward Viaduct should have been called the William Maclean Viaduct.

January 18, 2009

Historic "Snow Fight"

The abundance of snow that has fallen so far this winter has prompted the TTC to issue a warning to motorists. Vehicles that are parked on streetcar routes and obstruct the tracks will be ticketed and towed. No excuses.

Ray Corley photo courtesy of the John Bromley Archives.

Snow clearing techniques during Toronto's greatest twenty-four-hour snowfall (20 inches) included the use of one of its work cars equipped with a plough. In this view, W-1 is hard at work on Kingston Road near Victoria Park Avenue on December 13, 1944.

The conflict between snow and its obstruction of streetcar tracks is not a new phenomenon here in Toronto. Not by a long shot. In fact, one of the by-laws passed in 1861 that governed the operations of the city's first public transportation enterprise, the privately owned and operated Toronto Street Railway Company (TSR), had to do with snow and its accumulation on the various horse-drawn streetcar routes.

That by-law required that in the event of a heavy snowfall the company should attempt to keep its routes open, and if that was not possible it was to substitute horse-drawn sleighs (of which it had nearly one hundred) for its steel-wheeled vehicles.

While the intent of the by-law was obvious, it wasn't always adhered to by the company. That's because the sleighs were smaller than the regular streetcars and with fewer passengers on board there were fewer nickels in the company farebox.

One way to keep the bigger cars in service was to send out workers to clear the tracks of snow. But just like today, once the snow was removed from the streetcar tracks it had to be put somewhere, and that somewhere was usually in piles in front of the stores along the street.

An artist for the Canadian Illustrated News captured this "snow fight" between the crews of the horsecars operated by the Toronto Street Railway Co. and disgruntled store owners, the latter group aided by some enthusiastic young Torontonians. January 1881.

Often this would result in snow fights between the company men and the store owners.

One of the most serious of these confrontations occurred 128 years ago when a particularly heavy snowfall choked the city streets. The streetcar company insisted on using their large steel-wheeled cars, and to do so meant clearing the right-of-way down the centre of the street.

Out came the company men and their snow shovels and soon the tracks were clear, but now the sidewalks and store entranceways were impassable.

It wasn't long before the store owners, assisted by dozens of youngsters looking for something to do, began heaving the snow back onto the tracks. Soon snow throwing contests were going on all over downtown Toronto, and just when the store owners (and their assistants) looked as if they'd gotten the upper hand, the streetcar company shut the system down, the horses were unhitched and taken back to the stables, and for the next few days streetcars sat in the middle of the street surrounded by humungous snow banks.

Saner heads and warmer weather eventually combined to bring the transit crisis to an end.

January 25, 2009

Yorkville — the First 'Burb

When the name Yorkville comes up in conversation most people immediately think of the area in and around Bloor and Bay streets where many of the city's high-class boutiques, fashion stores, and restaurants can be found. Others will cast their memories back to the 1960s when Yorkville was home to hippies and Bohemians who would gather to listen to folk music in coffee houses such as the Inn on the

One of the earliest establishments in Yorkville was the Tecumseh Wigwam, a tavern located at the northwest corner of today's Bloor Street and Avenue Road. The Park Hyatt Toronto hotel now towers over the corner.

Courtesy of the Toronto Public Library.

William Botsford Jarvis and Joseph Bloor, co-developers of Yorkville, Toronto's pioneer suburb.

Parking Lot, the Half Beat, and The Mousehole.

But to local history buffs the term Yorkville means something completely different. Yorkville has the distinction of being Toronto's pioneer housing subdivision and the first of many communities to be annexed, which collectively have created today's modern City of Toronto. Interestingly, that historic act of annexation took place 126 years ago.

But let's go back to the beginning. At about the same time that the Town of York was elevated to the much more prestigious status of City of Toronto it was becoming obvious that increasing land prices within the newly created city were forcing people to look outside its boundaries for a place to build a home.

Taking advantage of this obvious business opportunity, two of the community's earliest settlers, Joseph Bloor (an English gentleman who had arrived in York in 1819, opened a popular hotel near the market, and eleven years later established a brewery in the valley northeast of today's busy Yonge-Church-Davenport intersection) and William Botsford Jarvis (one of the community's elder statesmen who had served as Sheriff of the Home District since 1827), acquired large parcels of land just outside the newly established city's northern boundary. The pair began selling off small lots on recently created side streets to Torontonians seeking a "new" life in the clean suburban air outside the city. Soon a few houses and shops began to appear, and by 1849 things were busy enough to prompt Henry Burt Williams, a carpenter and coffin maker, to open an omnibus line that connected the growing community with the city of some 25,000 souls to the south.

Meanwhile, Yorkville's population was approaching 1,000, a figure that the province had ruled was necessary for incorporation as a village. It's rumoured that to achieve that magic figure the names of some of the dear departed resting in the cemetery that stretched along the Concession Road (soon to be named in honour of Joseph Bloor) were added to the list.

This cemetery, known locally as Potter's Field, was the distant precursor of today's Mount Pleasant Cemetery. Potter's Field was to create problems limiting as it did Yorkville's future expansion. Public pressure eventually forced the old cemetery's closure in the early 1870s with all unclaimed remains removed to the recently established Necropolis and Mount Pleasant burial grounds.

Once the requisite number of inhabitants had been achieved the next step in the young community's evolution occurred on January 3, 1853, with the official incorporation of the new Village of Yorkville.

Over the following three decades the village saw large numbers of Torontonians move north opting to live and work in Toronto's first suburban community. However, this increase in population resulted in the inevitable. With insufficient funds to look after such necessities as a water supply, a proper sewage system, ongoing road maintenance, and sufficient fire and police protection, the village councillors were forced to ask the big city to assume those responsibilities. The city agreed, and on February 1, 1883, the Village of Yorkville vanished, joining the city as St. Paul's Ward and, as the new name suggested, it was now just another ward of the city.

February 1, 2009

Postcards from the Edge

Today millions of Canadians use electronic mail as a way of corresponding. Canadians of a century ago also corresponded back and forth, but relied on a much simpler method, the common picture postcard. To be sure, modern-day electronic mail (email or text messaging) is much faster, getting messages from my wireless phone or computer to yours at the speed of lightning. But in the early 1900s there was something special about waiting for the mailman to make his rounds and push that precious postcard through the mail slot in the door. Usually the news it carried was about family and friends, news that was more important than anything in that day's papers. And as a bonus, the hand-coloured photo on the other side of the card quite likely depicted some exotic Canadian or American attraction the sender was visiting.

Today, to include a photo with an email message you have to either embed it in the message or send it along as separate attachment. With the old-fashioned postcard, to see the image you simply turned the card over.

Also, to keep prying eyes from reading email messages one must use encryption codes or some other form of electronic authentication. To keep those old-fashioned postcards from being read by those who shouldn't, the sender merely writes the lines of text so they crisscross each other. Or, in some cases, simply writes the message upside-down

This postcard features a view of University Avenue looking north from Queen Street. Although the card bears no date research indicates it was taken sometime in mid-1911 since the 18-foot-high, two-ton bronze "Peace and Liberty" figure on top of the granite pillar wasn't put in place until the fall of that year.

Postcards don't have to be old to be collectible. This one features a view of Yonge Street south of Gerrard circa 1975. Note the once familiar A&A, Steeles Tavern, and Sam, the Record Man neon signs.

hoping that the mailman would be too busy to rotate the card so he could read it.

Oh and here's another difference between today's email messages and the old-fashioned postcard. Many of the latter have become fascinating (and sometimes valuable) collectibles. Not sure any of today's emails will achieve that status.

February 8, 2009

Casa de Toronto

It was soon after Toronto stockbroker Henry Pellatt married Mary Dodgson that the young couple moved into one of the many large houses that lined the east side of Sherbourne Street, south of Bloor. And it was while they were living here, in one of the finest residential areas in the city, that Henry's various business ventures began to pay off, especially those related to the sale of property in some of the recently developed areas of western Canada.

It wasn't long before these successes had transformed Henry Pellatt into one of the country's richest men. Now that he was among the nation's wealthy elite it was time to look for a new place to live, something more in line with Henry's new-found status in life. In 1903 he purchased the western portion of a large estate on the escarpment overlooking the modern Davenport-Spadina intersection.

Interestingly, Pellatt's new property, while still void of any buildings, had already been given the name Casa Loma by some anonymous developer. It would be here on the Casa Loma estate overlooking the City of Toronto that Henry would erect his new residence, one that would dwarf anything seen anywhere in the country.

Pellatt assigned the task of designing the new "house" to Edward James Lennox, one of the city's most prominent architects, whose recent projects — Toronto's new City Hall and Court House on Queen Street West (today's Old City Hall) and the magnificent King Edward

This postcard view shows both the Hunting Lodge and Sir Henry Pellatt's impressive stables just to the north of the castle. Both structures were built in 1905.

Hotel on King Street East — were still the talk of the town. However, since it would be years before Pellatt's massive new structure would be ready for occupancy, Henry decided to build a more conventional house on the estate.

Again he called on Lennox to design and build an interim residence, one that was to become known as the Hunting Lodge. It was located just south of the recently completed Pellatt stables and across the street from where the main residence would be constructed.

Sir Henry (who had recently been elevated to the status of Knight bachelor), Mary, and their son Reginald moved from 559 Sherbourne Street to the Hunting Lodge in 1906. It would be another seven years before Sir Henry and his wife were able to move into their still only partially completed home, a place they called Casa Loma.

Sadly, several financial setbacks resulted in the couple only being able to enjoy their palatial new home for less than a decade.

Many believed that this was because an unusually high property assessment figure placed on the property by the city and the resulting exorbitant property taxes made living in the castle prohibitive even for a man of wealth. Sound familiar? Eventually Casa Loma became the property of the city.

When the Pellatts finally moved into Casa Loma, the Hunting Lodge was left to Reginald who lived there with his wife until the son died in

QUEEN'S OWN RIFLES OF CANADA
TORONTO

Sir Henry Pellatt in his Queen's Own Rifles uniform sits astride one of his many horses.

1967. At this time the residence reverted to city ownership, which then leased it as a private residence. When that lease expired in 2008, the house again became part of the Casa Loma Estate.

February 15, 2008

Street Smart?

In the late 1800s–early 1900s annexation of the various small communities like Yorkville, Brockton, Riverdale, and North Rosedale not only resulted in Toronto growing larger in area and population, but the annexations presented a number of problems for municipal officials. Most obvious was the need to provide the new areas of the city with services such as clean water, sewers, and garbage disposal. Less serious perhaps, but no less important, was the confusion brought on by the increasing number of duplicated street names that resulted when many names in the newly annexed communities conflicted with existing city street names.

In most cases the duplicated names were simply descriptive words, names like Main, Church, Maple, Elm, or Centre. The easiest thing to do to correct the situation was to allow the older community (usually the City of Toronto) to keep its street names while replacement names were selected for duplicated street names that arrived with each newly annexed community.

However, this process wasn't always followed. In fact, a plethora of duplicate street names became a problem once again when in 1953 the twelve communities surrounding the City of Toronto, plus the city itself, merged to form the new Municipality of Metropolitan Toronto. This time some members of the new association of communities balked at giving up their street names and duplications again became a problem.

An interesting example of two Toronto streets with the same name is Leaside's Hanna Road and Hanna Avenue in Liberty Village, an emerging community located southeast of the King and Dufferin intersection. I've often wondered whether the similarity in names has caused emergency personnel problems. As to why the two names still exist, I can only assume that since each has a very special connection with the community in which that name is located the very idea of changing one or the other must have been met with considerable opposition. As a result, fire, police, or ambulance notwithstanding, nothing was done.

Interestingly, the two street names refer to two unrelated individuals with the same surname. In the case of the "Leaside Hanna," he was David Blythe Hanna. His importance stems from the fact that the residential community of Leaside actually began in the early 1900s as a model railway town developed by one of the country's transcontinental railways, the privately owned Canadian Northern. Hanna, who had arrived in Canada from Scotland in 1882, held numerous positions with this company and eventually became its vice-president. Then, when the government created

today's Canadian National Railway through the amalgamation of several bankrupt railways (including the Canadian Northern) Hanna was appointed the new railway's first president. His recognition by naming a Leaside street after him was an obvious choice.

The other Hanna refers to William John Hanna, who as Provincial Secretary in Premier Whitney's government oversaw asylums and

Right: David Blythe Hanna (1858–1938).

Below: Hanna Road street sign.

Anove: Hanna Avenue street sign.

Left: William John Hanna (1862–1919).

prisons. It was Hanna who, in 1915, forced the closure of Toronto's Central Prison, an appalling place that was located north of the CNE grounds and west of Strachan Avenue.

Nearby streets were named Hanna Avenue in honour of this prison reformer, while Liberty Street describes something eagerly sought and seldom achieved by many of the Central Prison inmates. Hanna replaced the Central Prison with new Ontario Reformatory in Guelph.

Incidentally, Ron Brown's book *Behind Bars* (Natural Heritage) describes in fascinating detail many of our province's pioneer jails, including Toronto's Don Jail and the Central Prison.

February 22, 2009

Big Time in History

One sure sign that spring is nearly here is the adoption of Daylight Saving Time (DST). By the way, did you remember to spring forward at 2:00 a.m.?

Interestingly, the concept of adjusting timepieces to take advantage of more daylight during the warmer months of the year goes back many centuries, but it was Englishman William Willett who, in 1905, made a plea to the government to seriously consider the issue, claiming it was unfortunate that golfers had to cut short their game because of darkness.

But, it was the onset of the Great War that really

Arguably, the most famous clock in the city is high up in the tower of "Old" City Hall, although in this view we see the tower prior to the clock being installed.

Old City Hall's four twenty-foot diameter "glazed skeleton" dials are among the largest in the world.

forced the issue with the Germans and their allies, introducing it first in 1916 and prompting other European countries, including Great Britain, to follow soon thereafter. On this side of the Atlantic the United States adopted DST in early 1918, with Canada following not long after.

Here in Toronto it was the city's popular mayor Tommy Church who notified his citizens that the Daylight Saving Law (the title by which it was identified in the newspaper ads) would go into effect at precisely 2 o'clock a.m., April 14, 1918. The notice ended with the traditional "God Save the King."

Of the hundreds of timepieces that had to be adjusted to comply with this new "law" one of the most obvious was the huge Gillett and Johnston instrument located several hundred feet above the Queen, Bay, and Teraulay intersection (the latter being the name of the extension of Bay north of Queen) in the tower of the city's nineteen-year-old City Hall. Today, the entire mechanism of what was officially identified in the manufacturer's catalogue as a "Number 5 Ting Tang" clock has been electrified, but in 1918 advancing the hands had to be performed manually. No simple task. Another adjustment had to be undertaken once the premier edition of Daylight Saving Time came to an end on Sunday, October 27. This time however, officials simply stopped the mechanism for sixty minutes.

March 8, 2009

Central Prison of Horrors

A couple of columns back I wrote about the origins of two similar Toronto street names, Hanna Road in Leaside and Hanna Avenue in the new Liberty Village community located southeast of the King and Dufferin intersection. The first street recognizes David Hanna, an official with the Canadian Northern Railway that created Leaside as a railway town, and the second, William Hanna, a senior official in the provincial government of Sir William Hearst and the man responsible for the closure of Toronto's outrageous Central Prison.

While most Torontonians know the history of the old Don Jail on Gerrard Street East (in fact, some know the jail better than others), few realize that we had another place of incarceration, the Central Prison.

Toronto's infamous Central Prison (from Dana William Ashdown's marvellous book *Iron & Steam, a History of Locomotive and Railway Car Builders of Ontario*, Robin Brass Studio).

Unlike the Don Jail which was looked after by the city, Central (as the place became known) was under provincial jurisdiction. This penal facility, located in an industrial area of the city far from the general public with the factories of Massey-Harris and the John Inglis Co. on nearby Strachan Avenue as its closest neighbours, greeted its first inmates in 1873.

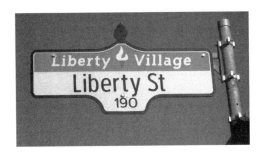

Liberty Street sign. This was the name given to the dirt pathway taken by prisoners when they were released from the Central Prison.

Central's initial mandate was to rehabilitate prisoners by keeping them busy with manual labour while giving them some sense of accomplishment. This was done by working out an arrangement with the nearby Canada Car & Manufacturing Co., which resulted in the inmates building rolling stock for the fast-growing railway freight business. The proximity of the Central Prison to several nearby railway corridors (that are still being used by GO Transit, Via Rail, and the CPR) made it easy to get these much needed box and platform cars to the railway companies in a hurry.

And in an effort to give the inmates some semblance of dignity, a small wage was paid to each man. In addition, the prison itself would receive money for manufacturing the rolling stock. This remuneration helped offset the cost of running the prison.

Unfortunately, the manufacturing company overextended itself financially and that, combined with the recession of the late 1870s (yes, there were others), led to the end of this innovative project. From then on inmates were kept busy manufacturing brooms and mops.

It was about this time that a new warden was placed in charge. He was an alcoholic ex-army officer and had a completely different method of "rehabilitating" inmates. Beatings became commonplace and requests for necessary medical treatment were conveniently misplaced. There were also rumours of secret early-hour burials outside the jail walls.

Before long, conditions in the Central Prison had become became so disgusting that provincial officials were forced to consider closing it. The man who made the ultimate decision was the Provincial Secretary, William Hanna, who is remembered in the name of a nearby street.

Toronto's Central Prison was closed in 1915, and its inmates transferred to the new reformatory in Guelph.

Today, only remnants of the Central Prison remain as silent reminders of those dark days from Toronto's castigatory past.

March 15, 2009

Motor Ride Back in History

Here's a question to keep in mind the next time you and a few friends are playing a friendly game of "Toronto Trivia." What's the connection between the name of a small residential street not far from the intersection of Coxwell and Cosburn Avenues and the trouble-plagued automobile empire we all know as General Motors? Here's a hint, the street is called Durant. Now what the heck has that name got to do with "The General"? And how did Durant get to be a Toronto street name anyway?

Here's the story. "Billy" Durant was born in Boston, Massachusetts, in 1861. After dropping out of high school he spent a short time as a cigar salesman. Then at the age of twenty-five he partnered with Josiah Dort, and together

Billy Durant, the founder of General Motors.

The assembly line at the Durant Motors factory on Laird Drive in Leaside.

they purchased the small, but profitable, Coldwater Cart Co. Using their considerable marketing skills it wasn't long before their enterprise had risen to become the largest carriage maker in the United States.

However, with the twentieth century only a few years old, Durant had become convinced that the future was no longer in the manufacturing of the old-fashioned horse-drawn carriages, but rather in the building of the modern horseless carriages. His vision was to create a multi-brand car consortium that he would call the International Motor Car Company. In mid-September of 1908, he incorporated his new company, although he selected a slightly different name. The new enterprise would be known as General Motors, William C. Durant, President.

The new company was less than two weeks old when it acquired its first brand, one that was the creation of Scottish-born inventor David Dunbar Buick and a vehicle that had become one of the most popular makes of the day. Next into the General Motors family came Ransom E. Olds' *Oldsmobile* followed by Henry Leland's *Cadillac* and then Edward Murphy's *Oakland* (a car that would eventually be replaced by the *Pontiac*).

Unfortunately, in 1910 the high flying Durant lost control of the company. Not daunted, he began purchasing other automobile companies, of which there were many. Quietly he began buying stock in the company he had founded, and by 1916 he was in charge once again. Durant held onto the presidency for another four years before being forced out once more. Never again would Billy Durant return to the company he had established in 1908.

Interestingly, it was during his second term as president that Durant brought the new Chevrolet (named for a prominent race car driver of the day, Louis Chevrolet) under the GM umbrella.

But it wasn't long before Durant's passion for automobiles again overtook him, and in 1921 he established a new car company. This one would be known as Durant Motors Inc. His new enterprise did well, producing large numbers of

Durant Street sign in East York

Durant and Star automobiles in the States. And to look after a growing Canadian and overseas market Billy established an assembly plant in a former munitions plant at the southeast corner of Laird Drive and McRae Avenue in the Toronto suburb of Leaside. In 1928 he constructed a new headquarters for Durant Motors of Canada right across the street from the factory. Now an office building, it still stands at 150 Laird Drive.

When Durant's American operations folded in 1932, just one of the hundreds of victims of the world-wide financial crisis that swept the world in the 1930s, several Toronto businessmen purchased his Canadian operation and kept things going as Dominion Motors Ltd. This company manufactured the popular Frontenac four and six cylinder automobiles. But, as popular as these cars were, they were up against a faltering economy and Dominion Motors went out of business in 1935.

William C. Durant died in 1947, but his name lives on in the title of a small street here in Toronto.

March 22, 2009

A Time for Talkies

There's been quite a bit in the media on the unfortunate turn of events that have impacted the reputation of one of the city's best known live entertainment organizations as well as that of two of its senior officials. However, despite what has befallen Garth Drabinsky we will always be indebted to him for the beautiful restoration of one of Toronto's most elegant buildings, the Pantages, now Canon Theatre on Yonge Street. This is the same building that for a time was a movie theatre known as the Imperial and later a multi-screen movie house called the Imperial Six.

While on the subject of theatres, Toronto has always been a "theatre city," and over the years has been home to such mammoth playhouses as the Hippodrome (2,386 seats) on Teraulay (now Bay Street) just north of Queen and the Tivoli (1,436 seats) at the southwest corner of the Richmond and Victoria intersection, as well as two theatres built by Marcus Loew. His downtown structure on the east side of Yonge north of Queen was called, naturally enough, Loew's (2,096 seats) while the one on the west side of Yonge just south of Bloor was Loew's Uptown (2,743 seats). Of this quartet, only the downtown Loew's remains as one half of the amazing Elgin and Winter Garden Theatre Centre.

By the way, and just to set the record straight, Pantages, in its incarnation as the Imperial Theatre, could seat 3,373 patrons, making it the largest theatre not just in our city but in the entire country. The Orpheum in Vancouver, with 2,871 seats, was next in size.

Of course, in addition to the large playhouses I've mentioned, Torontonians also had their choice of literally dozens of smaller theatres scattered throughout the city's various neighbourhoods. Many also featured both live performances in the form of vaudeville, as well as motion pictures, both silent and "talkies." Readers will doubtless have memories of attending theatres with such interesting names as Kum-C, Ace, Ideal, Classic, Doric, Kent, Circle, Pylon, Joy, Pix, and Village, the latter on Spadina Road, right in the heart of the Village of Forest Hill.

My wife Yarmila and I both spent our early years (though we actually didn't meet until many years later) in the Bathurst-Bloor-Harbord part of town where we had the Alhambra, Midtown, Bloor, and Metro (that at the time was a tiny movie house, not a giant grocery store) to choose from.

Shea's Theatre opened in 1910 and was demolished forty-six years later. The name recognizes its owners, Jerry and Mike Shea.

SHEA'S THEATRE

MATINEE DAILY 25c	WEEK OF MAR. 24	EVENINGS 25c, 50c, 75c

THOMAS A. EDISON'S
Latest and Greatest Invention

TALKING PICTURES

KAUFMAN BROS.
Black Face Comedians

PROVIDENCE PLAYERS
In "Who is Brown?"

MARY ELIZABETH
In Song and Story.

ZERTHOS DOGS
The Dogs of All Nations.

ALBERT VON TILZER
American Song Writer and Entertainer.

BLANCH SLOAN
"The Girl of the Air."

Special Easter Attraction

ROBERT T. HAINES & CO.
Presenting "The Coward"
A Play in One Act by George Broadhurst.

A 1913 newspaper ad promoting Thomas Edison's "talking pictures." They were being presented at Shea's Theatre at the southeast corner of Victoria and Richmond Streets in downtown Toronto. Shea's was one of Toronto's earliest vaudeville houses.

One of the larger playhouses that I've left until last is one that's no longer part of the city scene, but holds a special place in Toronto's theatre history. Shea's Victoria was located at the southeast corner of Victoria and Richmond. It was built by the Shea brothers, Mike and Jerry, in 1910, and at 1,140 seats was a substantially larger vaudeville house than the city's original Shea's Theatre on lower Yonge Street.

What makes Shea's Victoria unique is that it was in this theatre that Torontonians heard "talkies" for the very first time. This historic event took place a full sixteen years before Torontonians would be thunderstruck as they listened to Al Jolson's voice in *The Jazz Singer* reverberate throughout the Tivoli Theatre, the Victoria's neighbour just across the street.

However, it was on Monday, March 24, 1913, that Toronto theatre history was officially made when patrons visiting Shea's Victoria and having watched a somewhat ordinary vaudeville program were awestruck when the image of a man suddenly appeared on the theatre's silent movie screen and began to move his lips. Suddenly the audience could hear his voice! He proceeded to describe the principles behind inventor Thomas Edison's "talking pictures" invention. The sounds had actually been recorded on a disc and played back on a type of record player (Kinetophone) that was synchronized with the projector (a modified Kinetoscope) by means of cables and pulleys. The man's dissertation was followed by images and sounds of a piano recital and a portly vocalist and her rendition of "The Last Rose of Summer." Next came a violin solo followed by moving images of a group of dogs, and the audience could actually hear them bark! The event was electrifying and managed to fill the entire theatre for the rest of the week (except Sunday when church was the only source of "entertainment" permitted).

A fascinating description of the history of moving pictures in Toronto from 1894–1914 can be found in Robert Gutteridge's self-published book *Magic Moments*.

March 29, 2009

Original *"Mr. Fix-It"*

The other day my wife and I visited the Lowe's store in the city's west end. For anyone who's into major home renovating projects or simply looking for that illusive fluorescent light fixture (as we were) this place has got it all. And after an hour or more touring the miles of shelves and thousands of do-it-yourself products I had no doubt in my mind that Peter Whittall would have been tremendously impressed.

Now you may ask just who this fellow Peter Whittall was, anyway. Certainly, anyone who remembers watching early Canadian television on CBLT, Channel 9 (that's right, when the Toronto's first television station went on the air in it was to be found at that position on the dial — remember the television "dial"?) will recall the name Peter Whittall.

Peter was born in Toronto, but raised on a farm located some 100 miles north of Winnipeg. His first job was as a movie critic for a Winnipeg newspaper where he initially did reviews of westerns. After his first review, his subsequent reviews consisted of four words ... "Same story — different horses." His responsibilities were quickly changed. Since the newspaper didn't pay well, to supplement his income during the dismal years of the Great Depression Peter earned a few dollars as his neighbourhood's handyman.

The Whittall family moved back to Toronto in 1950 where Peter began his TV career soon after Canada's second TV station went on the air on September 8, 1952. (Montreal was first by just two days.) He was a

Peter Whittall, Canada's original "Mr. Fix-It."

frequent guest on a variety of local variety shows until 1955 when he was given his own fifteen minute slot at 6:30 every Saturday night. It wasn't long before his *Mr. Fix-It* program had grown to become one of the most popular shows on national television. At the peak of his popularity, Peter received more than 6,000 letters a week, and this was long before email. Dressed in his familiar plaid shirt and using home spun humour and the simplest of terminology he would explain to the viewers how to fix a leaking faucet, install a shelf, or make minor electrical repairs.

And don't forget, this was decades years before the arrival of Bob Villa, Tim "the Tool Man" Taylor, or PBS's popular *This Old House* show on PBS.

Canada's "Mr Fix-It" was a TV personality until health problems forced his retirement in 1965. Peter Whittall passed away October 12, 1974.

And while on the subject of do-it-yourself, it's been a few years now since we've been doing-it-ourselves separating recyclables from kitchen

Toronto's grey-blue-green bin, 1913-style. It was available from The Stove Store, 304 Queen Street West.

and other household wastes and placing each in the appropriate bin for curbside pickup. The newspaper ad accompanying this column shows that while Torontonians of nearly a century ago didn't separate their garbage they did have a special way of getting the stuff to the curb.

April 5, 2009

Tough Act to Follow

A couple of weeks ago I featured the story of the Shea's Victoria, a Toronto theatre that holds the distinction of being the first in the city to present a "talking" movie. The year was 1913 and that "talkie" was the creation of inventor Thomas Edison (who, by the way, would have been a Canadian had his father not been involved in the unsuccessful rebellion against the government of our province in 1837 and fled to Ohio to avoid capture and incarceration).

Other Toronto theatres have interesting histories as well. Take the other Shea's, the one called the Hippodrome over on Bay north of Queen. It was here that future comedy legend Red Skelton got his start as the emcee of a variety of vaudeville acts. And the 1920 Pantages on Yonge Street has evolved into today's Canon Theatre, while down the street the former Loew's Yonge Street (1913) and Winter Garden (1914) have been restored by the Ontario Heritage Trust into the amazing and unique Elgin Winter Garden Theatre Centre.

And then there was Murray Little's Casino Theatre.

Located on the south side of Queen Street, opposite a non-descript row of old buildings that would eventually be demolished for the present New City Hall, the 1,100 seat Casino opened at one minute after midnight Monday, April 13, 1936. The time is important since back then virtually all forms of entertainment were prohibited on Sunday.

In those early days the Casino presented a variety of burlesque acts

The Casino Theatre was located on Queen Street West, opposite where New City Hall stands today.

that featured jugglers, ventriloquists, and, dare I say it, strippers (imagine, strippers in staid old Toronto).

Often, an upstanding citizen would complain that these shows were not as wholesome as they should have been and demanded that the theatre be closed down. Complaints also would be presented to the members of the municipal council who met in what was the City Hall of the day just across and along the street from the theatre.

Those complaints never seemed to amount to much since they were directed at officials who were frequent opening night customers and in their eyes there simply wasn't anything wrong with the performances ... or the performers.

Motion pictures were an added feature at the Casino, and it has been suggested that some customers actually came to watch them.

But without doubt the heyday of the Casino occurred during the late 1940s–early 1950s when the weekly stage attraction was the appearance of some of the most popular American recording artists of the day. To list them all is beyond the scope of this column, but let me offer a few: Tony Bennett (his first Canadian appearance), Mel Tormé, Vic Damone, Connie Francis, The Platters, Bill Haley and his Comets, Hank Snow, Tex Ritter, Julius LaRosa, Johnny Ray, and Guy Mitchell. Especially popular were Toronto's own Four Lads and the Crew Cuts.

Eventually, the combination of television and the fantastic cash payments offered by the clubs in Las Vegas soon had the Casino and other similar theatres across the country left without headliners. The strippers made a comeback, but audiences had changed. In an attempt to fit in, the Casino changed its name in 1962 to the Civic Square (anticipating the redevelopment of the property across Queen Street) and began offering live theatre. That didn't work, and neither did another format change with the re-renamed Festival Theatre offering art films.

By 1965 it was all over for the old place, and soon it, as well as a couple of nearby hotels, a few small restaurants, a collection of pawnshops and second-hand stores (one of which was the original Henry's camera store), were demolished to make way for the new Sheraton Centre Hotel.

Barry Little, son of the Casino's founder Murray Little, is working on a book that will capture the hundreds of stories associated with his dad's fascinating theatre. I'll be sure to let readers know when copies are available.

April 12, 2009

Night Toronto Burned

It's a pretty safe bet that on April 19, 1904, there was a hot time in this old town. Let me explain.

It was a little after 8:00 p.m. that fire erupted in a small pile of combustible material left on a table located on the upper floor of the E & S Currie Company building located on the north side of Wellington Street just west of the York Street intersection. The material had been set aside for use the next day in the fabrication of men's neckties. What happened next was to change the face of downtown Toronto forever.

Though it started as a small fire, the fact that the staff had left earlier that day allowed the flames to grow in intensity, undetected. Soon a roaring blaze was consuming everything in its path. The intense heat caused the windows to explode, and in seconds the flames had jumped across the small laneway between the Currie building and the building next door to the east.

By now the fire was being fanned by cold, strong winds blowing in from the northwest. A bobby-helmeted police officer patrolling his beat up on King Street near the Bay Street corner saw the glow in the distance and quickly rang in an alarm using the nearby fire call box #12. Within minutes members of the city's fire department were on the scene. But by then most if not all of the buildings in and around the Wellington and York intersection were enveloped in flames. The seriousness of the situation was obvious.

Spectators view the remains of just a few of the more than one hundred buildings destroyed in the Great Toronto Fire that erupted 105 years ago.

Typical of the equipment available to fight fires in the early 1900s this Waterous pumper, photographed in front of the Lombard Street fire hall (the building is still there), was drawn by a trio of horses.

Over the next few hours and continuing well into the early morning hours of the next day the flames continued to devour more and more buildings. At the height of the conflagration the entire area from just south of King Street all the way to the shore of Toronto Bay (which at that time was just south of The Esplanade) and from near Yonge on the east to just beyond York Street on the west had been transformed from what had been earlier that day the bustling commercial heart of the city into a charred ruins crisscrossed by blackened and still sizzling telephone and telegraph lines and overhead streetcar wires.

Records indicate that more than two hundred city firefighters attended the blaze, plus many more from various outlying communities including several firemen and two steam pumpers, #12 and #13, that the Buffalo Fire Department sent by express train. In all, more than one hundred buildings housing 220 businesses were destroyed. Damage estimates exceeded $10 million (1904) and, perhaps worst of all, some 5,000 people were suddenly unemployed. There was even some suggestion that Toronto could no longer boast that it reigned as the province's commercial heart. That honour would now go to Hamilton.

As a direct result of the disaster the city fathers ordered that the existing low pressure water system, which became more and more useless as more and more streams of water were poured on the fames, be replaced by a high-pressure system, the same one that protects us today. And one other interesting reminder of the fire exists in the name of the volunteer organization that attends all major Toronto fires today. It's known as Box 12 in recognition of the fire call box on which that police officer rang in the initial alarm that cold April evening.

April 19, 2009

Full Steam Ahead

Does anyone happen to know how many times the federal government has floated the idea of a high speed train that would operate along the Quebec City–Windsor corridor? Perhaps a hundred would be overstating it. Nevertheless, the origin of inter-city train travel, in this part of the country at least, can perhaps be traced to an event that happened right here in Toronto 156 years ago.

It was on April 26, 1853, that the newly built steam locomotive *Toronto* was lifted off a pair of temporary rails and onto the recently laid tracks of the Ontario, Simcoe and Huron Railway, a title that was selected to identify the lakes that the new freight and passenger railway would serve. In another three weeks the *Toronto* would haul the first train to operate anywhere

In this somewhat fanciful sketch from the collection of Derek Boles, the newly built locomotive *Toronto* makes its way from James Good's Toronto Locomotive Works near the Yonge and Queen intersection to the Ontario, Simcoe and Huron tracks on the city's waterfront just south of Front Street. April 1853.

Mighty CN locomotive 6213, an attraction at Exhibition Place since 1960, the year after it was retired from service, will soon find a new home at the Toronto Railway Heritage Centre located in the historic CP Roundhouse just south of the CN Tower.

in the province from the city of its namesake northward to a community we now call Aurora. By early 1855 this route had been extended into the hinterland where it terminated at Collingwood on Georgian Bay.

Eventually the OH&S (called the "Oats, Straw and Hay" by its detractors) was renamed the Northern Railway, which then became part of the Grand Trunk Railway. The Grand Trunk was to become part of today's Canadian National system.

While it's almost impossible to comprehend today, the OH&S's locomotive *Toronto* was built in a foundry that was located just a few yards northeast of today's busy Yonge and Queen intersection. The proprietor of the foundry was James Good who had immigrated to this city from Dublin, Ireland, in 1832. Unfortunately for Good his early business ventures were thwarted by fires and bad debts, but by 1851 he was successfully manufacturing a variety of steam engines. One of Good's engines was installed in the new Toronto Island ferry boat *Victoria* thus making it the first vessel on Toronto Bay to be propelled by steam. Up until *Victoria*'s arrival every other vessel was quite literally horse-powered and by that I mean powered by real horses. Today, *Victoria*'s counterpart on the bay is *Trillium*, which will celebrate its centennial in June of next year.

Over the next few years James Good manufactured a total of 23 steam locomotives in his downtown Toronto foundry, nine for the OH&S and others for the Buffalo, Brantford and Goderich Railway, the Cobourg and Peterborough Railway and the Grand Trunk. However, financial problems including the availability of competitively priced, foreign-made locomotives (shades of the new TTC streetcar procurement process) eventually forced the Toronto businessman out of business. James Good died in 1889 and was buried in Mount Pleasant Cemetery.

Other non-railway uses were found for the factory until the property was redeveloped in the late 1800s.

A complete history of the numerous locomotive and railway car builders that were in business here in Toronto can be found in Dana Ashdown's fascinating book *Iron & Steam* (Robin Brass Studio).

April 26, 2009

John Lyle's Vision Shaped in T.O.

W hat do the two buildings shown in the photographs accompanying this column have in common? One view shows Toronto's magnificent Union Station a few years after it was finally opened to the general public. The other, a new branch of the Dominion Bank (renamed the Toronto-Dominion after amalgamating with the Bank of

Toronto's new Union Station as it appeared on a rare "real photo" postcard, circa 1934. Note the TTC's Peter Witt motor and trailer in the foreground. It operated on the Yonge route looping downtown at the southeast corner of Front and Simcoe Streets.

170

In this 1912 photo from the City of Toronto Archives a new branch of the Dominion Bank sits all by itself at the southeast corner of St. Clair Avenue (left) and Vaughan Road (foreground).

Toronto in 1955) that was built to serve the fast-growing community of Wychwood in and around the intersection of St. Clair Avenue and Vaughan Road. As dissimilar as these two buildings may appear, both bear the imprint of Canadian architect John Lyle whose career is the subject of a book published by Coach House Press. Titled *A Progressive Traditionalist*, this lavishly illustrated soft cover book traces the life and times of John Mackintosh Lyle from his birth in Ireland in 1872 and early life in Hamilton, Ontario. It goes on to cover Lyle's architectural training at several art schools in the States and at the École des Beaux-Arts in Paris, France. Returning to this side of the Atlantic he obtained employment with a variety of New York City architects and then moved to Toronto in 1905 where Lyle opened an office in a building just east of the recently-completed King Edward Hotel. While this book would be a welcome addition to any architect's library, those of us who are interested in less specific aspects of our city's history will also find the book great reading, incorporating as it does many of John Lyle's creations that we see every day. A few examples, the Runnymede Branch of the Toronto Public Library on Bloor Street West, the Royal Alexandra Theatre on King Street West, and the Bank of Nova Scotia at the northeast corner of King and Bay Streets.

Interestingly, Lyle's design for this latter building had actually been completed prior to the onslaught of the Great Depression. Money concerns put the project on hold, but with the Second World War successfully concluded work on the bank's new Head Office began once again. And even though architect Lyle had passed away, bank officials still regarded his plans perfect for their new building. Those plans were simply dusted off and updated, and soon Toronto had a striking new skyscraper, another Lyle masterpiece.

May 17, 2009

Royal Reception

About seventy years ago Torontonians were still talking about one of the most exciting events they had ever witnessed. Just two days earlier, May 22, 1939, their beloved Monarch, King George VI, accompanied by his Queen, had undertaken a whirlwind eight-and-a-half-hour tour of the city as part of their historic trip across Canada. The couple's train, pulled by CPR's mighty locomotive 2850, arrived at 10:30 a.m. at the CPR's North Toronto railway station on Yonge Street, a few blocks south of St. Clair Avenue. That station has been beautifully restored and now serves as a LCBO store.

First on the Royal itinerary was a massive public reception at Toronto City Hall. They were met by Mayor Ralph Day who led the crowd in a rousing cheer for their Majesties. It was then off to the Parliament Buildings with the five vehicle entourage using a routing that took the couple south on Bay, west on Front then north up University Avenue. All along the way buildings and light standards were draped with Union Jacks and colourful red, white, and blue bunting. At Queen's Park their Majesties met Premier Mitchell Hepburn, his provincial ministers, and senior officials before resting in Lieutenant Governor A.E. Mathews' suite. They then made their way to the nearby University of Toronto campus where the Royal Couple (and several hundred invited guests) lunched at Hart House. On the way, the Queen presented new colours to her regiment, the Toronto Scottish.

Huge crowds gather in front of City Hall to welcome King George VI and Queen Elizabeth during the couple's one-day visit to Toronto, May 22, 1939.

It was now 2:30 in the afternoon and the procession was on the move again with a short trip north to Bloor Street, a slow right turn, and within minutes the motorcade was speeding across the Bloor-Danforth Viaduct. As they did there's little doubt that someone in the car explained to them that the massive bridge was named twenty years before after the King's older brother, Edward, the Prince of Wales (thus the official name of the structure, the Prince Edward Viaduct).

Next was a half-hour stop in Riverdale Park where thousands of school children and their parents had gathered to cheer the King and Queen. By 3:30 p.m. they were in their seats at Woodbine race track on Queen Street East (a street named to honour the King's great-grandmother, Victoria, although I'm not sure whether they explained that to George).

The reason for the visit to the track was to witness the eightieth running of the Queen's/King's plate, the actual title of the race depended on who the reigning monarch was at the time. A little Toronto trivia, that particular trophy and the 50 guineas (sovereigns) was won by "Archworth" ... by ten lengths.

Following the historic race the city tour continued with the motorcade returning to Queen's Park along crowd-lined Queen and King Streets, (the latter named for the great, great, great grandfather of the King), turning north up University Avenue to the Parliament Buildings where the couple rested once again in the lieutenant governor's suite before a circuit of the city's west end.

Their first stop on this part of the visit was at the Military Hospital on Christie Street where they met many veterans of the Great War. Then it was west out Bloor Street, down Parkside Drive to the Lake Shore Boulevard and east to the Grandstand in the CNE grounds, where thousands of spectators roared their collective welcome.

By now it was well after 6:00 p.m., and if the tight schedule was to be met the short trip to Union Station had to be a quick one.

Arriving at the station a little before 7:00 p.m. the King and Queen boarded their train (pulled by CNR locomotive 6400) and soon this historic visit would be over. It would turn out to be the one and only visit to Toronto by King George VI, while Elizabeth would return on several occasions in the future.

May 24, 2009

The Dating Game

One of the most frequently reproduced photographs showing a much earlier Toronto is the one featured in this column. It captures, with spectacular clarity, a huge crowd gathered on Yonge Street just north of King. Over the years this photograph has appeared as a postcard, in various books and in numerous newspaper articles. What's interesting is that the view, though always identified as "Yonge Street looking north from King" frequently bears one of two dates, either 1900 or 1902. Which one is correct?

One thing we do know for sure is that the crowd is celebrating some event related to the South African (or Boer) War, a conflict that lasted from October 1899, until May 1902. We also know that the photographer was Alexander Galbraith (1867–1950), this latter fact being a much easier determination since his name appears at the lower right corner of the original photo.

The specific date that the photo was taken is a little more difficult to determine. It is often identified as crowds celebrating the end of the war, a much anticipated event that was finally concluded with a peace treaty signed on May 31, 1902. However, close inspection of the various company signs seen in the view precludes the year 1902, since many of the names do not appear in the 1903 City Directory (the 1903 directory listed all the businesses on Yonge Street the previous year, 1902).

More likely the year in question is 1900 as the vast majority of those businesses in the view are in the 1901 directory. As for the actual date

Alexander Galbraith took this amazing photograph of jubilant crowds celebrating a British victory during the South African War. While the actual date of this photo is unknown it's quite possible it was taken on May 31, 1900, following the Relief of Pretoria.

Yonge Street looking north from King to Adelaide, May 2009.

in 1900, perusal of the contemporary city newspapers revealed that on June 1 feature stories describing the massive crowds that had gathered on Yonge Street to celebrate what was being called the Relief of Pretoria filled all editions. Headlines such as "A Delirium of Rejoicing" and "Great Demonstration on Yonge Street" would suggest that Galbraith's remarkable photograph was taken on May 31, 1900, a date that would be identified forever as Pretoria Day.

Sadly, as jubilant as the crowds may have been on that warm day in May, the war would actually go on for another two years. A total of 244 Canadians died either in battle or of diseases they had contracted during the hostilities. Their sacrifice is recognized with Walter Allward's impressive memorial at Toronto's Queen Street and University Avenue intersection.

May 31, 2009

Ahead of its Time

L ast week I hosted a day-long bus tour around our great city with a
seniors' group from Pickering. One of the sites we visited was the
Legislative Buildings of Ontario where the knowledgeable staff always
present a fascinating look at the history of the "pink palace," a spectacular
building that opened in 1893 and was constructed for a miniscule (in
today's terms at least) less than $1.25 million. When the government is
in session this part of the visit is followed by a half-hour or so of watching
members of the government go at it with the loyal opposition.

While I waited in front of the building for the group to complete its
tour I watched as government officials were given rides in a bright blue
Ford Fusion that Frank Stronach's Magna International had converted
from its hybrid configuration (with both gasoline and electric motors) to
a single power source all-electric vehicle. My guess is that this is the type of
automobile Magna is hoping to build right here in Ontario.

But what struck me as I watched as this demonstration was just how
quiet this vehicle was as it glided by. And more importantly, during the
entire time that Frank's Fusion was being demonstrated not one drop
of gasoline was consumed, making the vehicle more environmentally
friendly than any hybrid on the market today.

As I watched the goings on I suddenly had the urge to tell the
assembled crowd a fascinating fact about Toronto's own automobile
history. However, before I could my group emerged from the building and

This sketch depicts owner Fred Fetherstonhaugh at the controls of his all-electric "horseless carriage." It was the very first automobile seen on the streets of Toronto.

began boarding the bus. Oh well, those big shots would just have to wait to hear my story or maybe they might just read here in the *Sunday Sun*.

While Mr. Stronach's concept of an all-electric vehicle is fascinating, it certainly wasn't the first time this type of vehicle was seen here in our city. In fact, the very first "horseless carriage" to operate on the streets of Toronto was ... wait for it ... an all-electric. Built by the city's pre-eminent patent attorney, Frederick Barnard Fetherstonhaugh, his one-of-a-kind motorized carriage made its first appearance on Toronto city streets in the fall of 1896.

At its heart was a small electric motor described by the owner as of the "disc armature type, six polar with the field being series wound." It was supplied by current from a specially designed "lead paste-type battery" was had been developed by local electrician W.J. Still. It was made up of thirty-six individual cells that resulted in a large battery with a total weight of nearly 850 pounds. It was said that when fully charged this battery would give Fetherstonhaugh's electric carriage a range of nearly 30 miles.

⊣ EATON'S ⊢

The Waverley Electric Limousine---
Just Arrived in Toronto

The silent "Full View Ahead" electric touring car is here! Just come to us from its makers, the Waverley Company, at Indianapolis. This company has had sixteen seasons of electric carriage building! Think what that means—and the 1912 Silent Waverley Electric Car is the product of the experience gained in those sixteen years. As a town car, the Waverley Electric is unexcelled. See its advantages.

It seats five grown-ups comfortably.

It gives the driver absolute command of the road.

It may be driven by a chauffeur or a member of the family with equal ease and propriety.

It costs less to maintain than any gasoline car.

It is characterized by beauty of design, elegance of appointment and thoroughness of workmanship. The Silent Waverley Electric Limousine embodies the most important innovation in motor carriage construction of recent years, viz. —an **Inside Driven Closed Car with the Driver Occupying the Front Seat**—That is what is meant by the phrase "Full View Ahead." After that, perhaps the most striking feature of the design is its low centre of gravity, which gives both the reality and the appearance of great stability to the Limousine.

Call and see the Waverley Electric at the Showrooms, Albert Street, or write for literature.

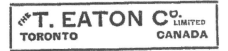

Eaton's department store began offering the Waverley Electric Limousine to its customers in 1912. Manufactured in Indianapolis, the car sold for nearly $4,500 and could be seen (and purchased) at the Eaton showroom on Albert Street just across the street from City Hall.

For the next few years the young patent attorney could often be seen cruising the less than smooth roads in and around Toronto in his revolutionary vehicle. He would often drive to his office in the old Bank of Commerce Building on King Street West in the heart of the city from his suburban residence, Lynne Lodge, located on the Lake Ontario shoreline at the foot of today's Royal York Road.

Actually, this location was perfect being as it was on the radial streetcar line. Using another electrical contraption, the inventor Fred Fetherstonhaugh was able to draw electricity from the company's overhead trolley wire and then modify it so it could be used to recharge his carriage's batteries.

Now whether the radial company knew he was doing it, that's another question.

While Fetherstonhaugh's marvel was the first, it wasn't long before other electric vehicles were seen all over town. One of the pioneer companies was Parker's cleaners who used electric wagons to speed up deliveries. Department store magnate John Craig Eaton has several electric vehicles and even began selling them at the company store.

One of the drawbacks faced by these early electric vehicles still faces the car industry: batteries that can provide enough power to get from here to there, as the distance to "there" becomes greater and greater. But that'll come.

June 7, 2009

Sky's the Limit

Toronto's ever-changing skyline started with one true landmark.

Anyone who spends any time these days studying the Toronto skyline will have certainly noticed the amazing changes that have occurred over a relatively short period of time. While once dominated by soaring skyscrapers owned by the mighty banks, today a proliferation of new condominium towers has taken over. The new skyline is a blur.

However, there was a time when the appearance of one new building on what had been a rather stagnant skyline prompted people to marvel and many to question where will it all end.

The building in question was CPR's new Royal York Hotel, one of our city's true landmarks that was officially opened eighty years ago by Canada's Governor General of the day, Viscount Willingdon, in the presence of the new hotel's godfather, CPR President E.W. Beatty.

The new CPR hotel was erected at a cost of $18 million (1929) on the north side of Front Street. Quickly obliterated to accommodate the massive new structure was another famous city hostelry, the Queen's, which though sadly outdated, continued right to the end to be regarded as one of the city's most charming.

For the next two years the Royal York had the skyline to itself, only to be upstaged in 1931 by the new thirty-four storey Bank of Commerce. This newcomer was identified as the tallest building in the entire British Commonwealth. It lost that title in 1962 with the opening of Place Ville Marie

For many years Toronto's skyline was dominated by just two buildings, the Royal York Hotel, at left, and the Bank of Commerce Building, right. The first was completed eighty years ago this year, the latter a mere two years later. Notice the CNR's steam locomotive hauling a freight train across the waterfront. It is the same type as the locomotive recently moved to the roundhouse near the CN Tower.

in Montreal. Toronto regained the title in the mid-1970s when the seventy-two storey First Canadian Place opened at the King at Bay intersection.

June 14, 2009

TORONTO, THURSDAY, JUNE 30, 1927   **5 O'CLOCK EDITION**   TWO CENTS

:S FROM LAND'S END AT 8 A.M.

C.P.R.'s "Royal York" Replaces Historic Queen's

ROYAL YORK IS CHOSEN NEW C.P.R. HOTEL NAME ROOM FOR 7,000 PEOPLE

President E. W. Beatty Selects Name for New Front Street Hotel Because of Historic Association—To Have Most Notable Floor in America

WILL TOWER 28 STORIES UP FROM GROUND VIEW OF BAY AND CITY FROM ROOF GARDEN

Toronto's new Canadian Pacific hotel will be known as "The Royal York."

After consideration of many suggested names President E. W. Beatty finally decided upon that as being most fitting, in that it associates the new hotel with the history of Toronto and conforms with the dignity and splendid appointments.

Work in preparation for the actual construction is going forward rapidly. The general design of the building and the arrangement of the public rooms have been approved by Mr. Beatty after some months of continuous work on the part of the architects and the company's engineering department.

28 Stories and Roof Garden

The result is a building that, besides being an ornament to the city of Toronto in every respect worthy of that city's importance and assured future growth, will be the largest and finest hotel building in the British empire, containing over 1,000 rooms, and so the front rank with the world's best. In general style its architecture will follow classical lines modified to meet the requirements of the building's purpose. Through a series of varying roof levels its central portion will

rise to a height of 28 storeys from the ground, carrying an upward sweep of graceful lines, under the crown of which will be a roof garden with facilities for entertainment and equipment for service taking up practically two floors.

It is likely that the building will be faced with grey stone, although that detail has not yet been definitely decided upon. In any case it will extend 350 feet along the north side of Front street opposite the new Union Station. Front street at this point is unusually wide, and as the station is well set back from the roadway the new hotel will be set off to splendid advantage. It will extend to York street on the west, to Piper street on the north and to an open space on the east. The rotunda and hotel lobby will be located in the centre of the building, reached by the main entrance from Front street and also from entrances on the east and west ends. Around this lobby will be placed the hotel offices, news and cigar stands, check rooms, writing room, cafe and a central bank of ten elevators. From the rotunda a foyer leads to a large lounge on one side and to the main dining room on the other. This will extend almost entirely across one end of the building. The service rooms and the kitchen will be on the Piper street front. Below this on the street floor will be an arcade extending from York street straight through to the east side of

LARGEST HOTEL IN BRITISH EMPIRE TO BE BUILT BY C.P.R.
Immediately after the Toronto hotel to stand on the site of the by the firm of Jacques and Hay many exhibition the C.P.R. will begin the tear-historic old Queen's. The famous years ago will also be preserved. The ing down of the old Queen's hotel and "Red Room" in the Queen's is to be vacant lot in the east of the present the erection of the fine new "Royal reproduced as faithfully as possible in hotel will also be used as part of the York" which is the name chosen by the new building, and some of the fine site of the new building, which is to President E. W. Beatty for the 1,000-old furniture and woodwork produced be completed at the beginning of 1929.

The June 30, 1927, edition of the Telegram newspaper was the first to announce the name of the city's mammoth new hotel. It also featured an architect's sketch of what this thing called the "Royal York" would look like.

Pomp and Pageantry

Several weeks ago I featured a photo in this column taken by pioneer city photographer Alexander Galbraith. It showed Yonge Street jammed with hundreds of Torontonians out celebrating an event that

June 22, 1897, and the intersection of King and Yonge streets is crowded with Torontonians celebrating Jubilee Day, the sixtieth anniversary of Queen Victoria's ascension to the throne. Note the portrait of the Queen on view on the front of the streetcar.

Courtesy of the City of Toronto Archives.

Queen Victoria gets a cleaning. The statue had quite a trip before finding a home in front of the east wing of the Legislative Buildings of Ontario.

was known as Pretoria Day. Many believed that as a result of the British victory over the Boers at Pretoria, the capital of the Transvaal, what had become known as the South African War was almost over. Unfortunately, those celebrations were premature. The war went on for another two years, eventually concluding on May 31, 1902.

Five years before those Pretoria Day celebrations Torontonians had also filled Yonge Street for another momentous event. This time it was in recognition of the sixtieth anniversary of Queen Victoria's ascension to the throne. Known as Jubilee Day, June 22, 1897, was filled with parades, musical performances, sporting events, and military demonstrations. Contemporary newspapers recorded for posterity that "the citizens had never seen anything like it." And what do you know;

there to capture a moment in time during those festivities was the same Alexander Galbraith. He had positioned the lens of his mammoth glass plate camera to look east along King Street from a vantage point just west of the crowded Yonge intersection.

Galbraith went on to capture numerous other photos of a much earlier Toronto. He died in 1950 and is buried in the Thornhill Cemetery. Sure wish I had met him.

By the way, anyone who has visited the Parliament Buildings at Queen's Park will know that Queen Victoria is present in our city in the form of a huge 9-foot-high bronze statue that weighs in at 5,600 pounds and was created by Italian sculptor Mario Raggi, who opened a studio in London about 1875.

While the statue was originally destined for a place of prominence at the top of today's University Avenue, according to Helen Nolan in her book *Sculpture in the City: Twelve Walks in Downtown Toronto* there wasn't enough money to pay for the work and as a result it remained in England. In fact, it wasn't until the public's sentiment had increased sufficiently following the beloved monarch's death in 1901 that enough money was raised and her statue returned to our city.

By then, however, the statue's proposed location had been usurped by Sir John A. Macdonald who has been standing there surveying University Avenue since his likeness arrived in 1894. So a new site was selected, and on September 22, 1902, while Premier Ross and other officials looked on, Victoria was placed in her present location. For some unexplained reason there was no official unveiling ceremony.

June 21, 2009

Keeping Us Amused

On June 28, 1922, the new Sunnyside Amusement Park located on the Lake Ontario shoreline opposite the foot of Roncesvalles Avenue was officially opened by the mayor of the day, Alfred McGuire. Destined

Access to the city's new Sunnyside Amusement Park, located on the Lake Ontario waterfront at the foot of Roncesvalles Avenue, was easy even if one didn't have a car. The TTC streetcars carried visitors to the door. The fare was 7 cents for adults, 4 cents for children.

If you were lucky enough to own a car the parking was plentiful and free. The Turrett cigarette sign overlooks the busy King, Queen, Roncesvalles, and Lake Shore intersection. Visible to the extreme left is the now vanished bridge that connected the corner with the Lake Shore Boulevard seen in the foreground.

to become one of the city's most popular summertime attractions the sprawling amusement park — with its fabulous rides, mouth-watering restaurants and snack bars, exciting games, and music-filled dance-halls — was destined to be obliterated in the mid-1950s by the much-anticipated Waterfront Expressway. Today we know this elevated highway as the Gardiner.

While little remains of good, old Sunnyside today, we can be thankful for the ongoing existence of the park's original bathing pavilion, its swimming tank (now renamed the Sunnyside/Gus Ryder Pool), and the lovingly restored Palais Royale.

Over our city's long history (a total of 175 years thus far) Torontonians have had the pleasure of visiting a lengthy list of amusement parks. One of the first of these opened in 1843 over on the Island which at the time was still connected to the mainland by a narrow strip of land at its easternmost end. These so-called "pleasure grounds" sat adjacent to a hotel operated by Peter and Louis Privat. The hotel itself had been opened a decade earlier and subsequently purchased by the brothers. With the addition of an amusement park, one that included a ten-pin bowling alley, swings, a hand-powered merry-go-round, plus a small zoo, the site quickly gained in popularity.

The brothers decided to take advantage of their property's new-found popularity by making it easier for potential customers to cross the bay. They enlarged the original ferry boat that was propelled by a pair of horses trotting on a treadmill connected to side paddles by adding three more horses. These two vessels were the precursors to Toronto's present Island ferry fleet.

A half-century later a much larger amusement park opened at the west end of the Island. In addition to a collection of traditional rides, games of chance, a dance hall, and fast food stands, Hanlan's Point Park also featured a series of large sports fields where Toronto's professional baseball team, the Maple Leafs of the Triple A minor league played until moving to the mainland stadium at the foot of Bathurst Street in 1926.

Other parks where Torontonians were able to relax and have fun included the pioneer Victoria Park, Munro Park, and Scarboro Beach Park, all located on the lakefront close to the city's eastern boundary. Of the three, Scarboro Beach Park was the most popular. It saw its first guests in 1907, but after many years of welcoming happy crowds it began to wither following the opening of the much more accessible Sunnyside Amusement Park far to the west.

Scarboro Beach Park closed following a less-than-successful 1925 season and the property soon cleared. Many of the houses that now stand south of Queen Street between Leuty and Maclean Avenues were constructed on the site of one of the city's many pleasure parks.

June 28, 2009

Streetcar City

It wasn't easy, but after months of meetings documents have been signed that will ensure Toronto retains its title of "streetcar city," a fact that has been part of Toronto's identity since the privately owned Toronto Street Railway Company placed its first horse-drawn public transportation vehicles into service up and down a dusty Church Street on September 11, 1861.

The first prototypes of Toronto's new generation streetcar, the final assembly of which will take place at the Thunder Bay factory of Bombardier, are scheduled to arrive in town in 2011.

The last of the 204 vehicles should be in service by 2018. In addition, it's likely that several hundred vehicles for the proposed "suburban" Transit City project will be built using many of the features of the "city" streetcar.

Of course, this isn't the first time the TTC has purchased new streetcars.

Soon after its creation by the provincial government in 1920, money came from both the city and province to assist Toronto's new publicly owned transit commission with the purchase of a large number of modern new steel streetcars (known as Peter Witts in recognition of the Cleveland transit expert responsible for their modern design).

These cars, each costing $17,000, would quickly replace the uncomfortable, inefficient and, in many cases, unsafe wooden streetcars that had been operated by the TTC's immediate predecessor, the privately owned Toronto Railway Company.

TORONTO DAILY STAR

T.T.C. BUYS 140 STREET CARS FOR $3,000,000

FAST, SILENT TROLLEYS BOUGHT WITH RESERVES IN OPERATION BY FALL

Now where have I recently read a headline similar to the one that appeared in the April 8, 1938, edition of the *Toronto Daily Star*? A few old Toronto PCCs still live, the one below as a restaurant near the community of Primrose, northwest of the city.

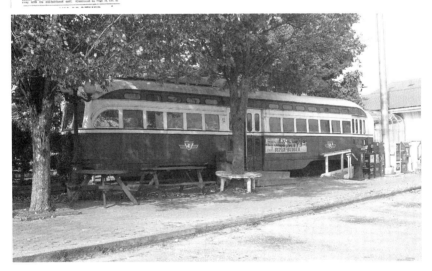

The public's acceptance of the new Toronto Transportation Commission (Transportation became Transit with the opening of the first section of Yonge subway in 1954) was immediate, with many thousands riding the much expanded and improved system every day.

In an effort to stay "ahead of the curve" (not something they'd say back then, but you know what I mean), senior staff of the TTC joined with staff of several other large North American transit companies to help develop a new streetcar, one that would eventually replace the TTC's aging fleet.

The result of this international project was an ultra-modern vehicle to be identified as the "Presidents' Conference Committee Streamliner," or simply the PCC. Initially, interest in purchasing this new streetcar was not overwhelming and it wasn't until the TTC put in its request for 140 of the new cars that the future of the PCC was assured.

Over time, the Commission purchased 540 new and 205 second-hand PCCs for a total of 745, one of the largest PCC fleets in the world. While the last one ran in regular service here in Toronto in December of 1995, two are still made available by the TTC for charters.

An interesting fact concerning the TTC's initial order for 140 new PCC cars is that they cost the Commission $3 million, or approximately $21,500 each, with none of that money coming from the city, the province, or the federal government (not sure if John Baird was around back then). The total order was paid for out of the TTC's surplus account.

And perhaps even more surprising, the deal was done without the approval of city council. Such was the status of the TTC in 1938.

July 5, 2009

Toronto in the Dumps

T his column is garbage, or should I say *about* garbage. From our community's earliest days a couple of centuries ago the collection and disposal of what was more delicately called back then "street sweepings"

Toronto's garbage disposal technique, 1954-style. Here a new, specially designed city garbage truck helps create a new landfill adjacent to the Humber River in Swansea.

and "refuse" was a minor inconvenience. Collection and burying was a fact of life. Many people looked forward to the cold winter months when the disposal of all sorts of unwanted material became even easier. The stuff was simply placed on the ice that usually covered the bay and when that ice eventually disappeared so, too, did the citizens' problems.

As the city grew in both size and population garbage collection and subsequent disposal became an ever-increasing problem. To help out more and more horses and carts were added to aid with the collection. The disposal problem became easier, and even profitable, by simply creating new land using the garbage as fill. This method was used along the old shoreline of Toronto Harbour and adjacent to the city's rivers and ravines. The waterfront in particular became a prime site for disposal, not just for tons of the city's street sweepings but for anything that would take up space: from household garbage, to chunks of demolished buildings, to other construction (or deconstruction) materials, and even to the old abandoned sailing vessel as shown in the photo accompanying this column.

Eventually, and in an effort to decrease the volume of materials to be disposed of, Toronto constructed four huge incinerators around the city. They included one on Commissioners Street in what's known today as the Portlands. It was the most modern of its kind when officially opened in April of 1955. Others were located on Wellington Street West, north of the CNE grounds (opened in 1925), on Symes Road (1934), and on the east bank of the Don River near Dundas Street (1917).

Toronto's new waterfront evolved out of dump sites that included not just garbage but in this case at the foot of York Street an abandoned sailing vessel.

The collected trash would be dumped into the incinerators' huge coal-fired furnaces where materials of all kinds would be reduced by the intense heat to inert matter, most of which would receive its final disposal as "inert" landfill somewhere around the city. Years later the supposed inertness of this material as well as the gases escaping from the incinerator chimneys would prove to be problematic. As a result, incineration, in the old fashioned way, is no longer practiced.

Will incineration in a new and safer form as used in other parts of the world make a return? Surveying the thousands and thousands of plastic garbage bags piling up across the city (except in Etobicoke, and to think we nearly moved there) it's obvious something has to be done. It's only been four weeks and pretty soon there won't be a hole big enough anywhere in the province to take it all.

On a brighter note, were you aware that those same plastic garbage bags that are tarnishing the city's neighbourhoods and reputation are the brainchild of a pair of Canadian inventors, Harry Wasylyk and Larry Hansen? These two sold their patent rights to Union Carbide. Had I known the garbage strike would last this long I would have invested in the company's stock. Come on somebody, do something!

July 19, 2009

*When this article was written, a garbage strike was in effect. It lasted six weeks (June 22–July 31, 2009) and was the longest in Toronto's history.

Here She Is, Miss Toronto (1926)

As the city goes about the job of trying to clean itself up by getting rid of the thousands of tons of garbage that should never been allowed to accumulate in parks, laneways, and on street corners in the first place I thought it was time to discuss something, well, prettier. And what better topic than the history of the Miss Toronto competitions that used to be an annual city event. In fact, for years they were part of the annual Police Games sponsored by the department's Amateur Athletic Association. However a little research reveals that the very first person tagged with the title "Miss Toronto" was fifteen-year-old Oakwood Collegiate schoolgirl Norma Niblock who was selected in a 1923 beauty contest held at Mutual Arena.

This event was really nothing more than a marketing plan to sell a face cream called Mineralava Beauty Clay. What made the contest so popular was that the emcee of the Arena show was none other than greatest silent movie super-star of the day Rudolph Valentino. Interestingly, Valentino's wife Winifred was the stepdaughter of Richard Hudnut, the cosmetic king. At the time of the contest Winifred was running the cosmetic company.

Norma was named "Miss Toronto," and in November of 1923 she and 87 other winners from cities across the States and Canada were paraded up New York City's 5th Avenue following which they all appeared at the old Madison Square Gardens. It was at this so-called "contest of contests" that the Toronto girl was awarded first prize.

The winner of the first "real" Miss Toronto competition held at Sunnyside Amusement Park on August 14, 1926, was Jean Ford Tolmie seen here (left) with runners-up Ellis Fitzgerald (centre) and Dorothy Asling (right).

However, the local papers must have regarded the whole thing as nothing more than a promotional gimmick to help sell face cream, and as a result virtually nothing was written about the young Toronto girl's accomplishment. And while the ads suggested that her prize would be a starring role in Valentino's next movie, that doesn't seem to have been the case. In fact, we don't have any idea what Norma won.

It wasn't until 1926 that the first "non-commercial" Miss Toronto was chosen, although the event was really a "come and visit our park and spend some money" promotion put on by the management of the four-year-old Sunnyside Amusement Park. The winner was Jean Ford Tolmie who, fearing her father would be upset that she had entered in the first place, used her mother's maiden name and signed the entry form as Jean Ford. She won the title and $200 over 454 entries.

For whatever reason, no similar contests were held until 1937 when the Toronto Police Amateur Athletic Association stepped in and decided to add something special to its annual Police Games, which had been ongoing since 1883. The event was held at the CNE grounds and this time the title of Miss Toronto went to seventeen-year-old Billie Hallam. Her prize was also $200.

An interesting feature of the 1937 edition of the Police Games was a door prize to be won by a lucky boy or girl who held the winning admission ticket. The prize, a donkey and cart, was donated by A.W. Miles, a Toronto undertaker and owner of Miles Zoo on the Dundas Highway west of the city. I can hear it now — "Hey mom! Look what I won!!"

The last police-sponsored Miss Toronto contest was held in 1992. A little Toronto trivia: her name? Julianne Gillies.

August 2, 2009

University's Magnificent Beacon

A nyone who travels Toronto's University Avenue cannot help but be impressed with the magnificent Canada Life Building located on the west side of the street just north of the Queen Street intersection. The company had been established in Hamilton, Ontario, in 1847 where business was good. But things could be better and it wasn't long before company officials decided to take advantage of the possibilities afforded by opening a small office on King Street West, right in the heart of the provincial capital Toronto.

The plan worked, and before long unprecedented growth made it necessary for the company to seek even larger premises. A new building was the only answer and it was into this six-story structure at 40–46 King Street West, soon known far and wide as the Canada Life Building, that the company Head Office was relocated in 1900.

Throughout the teens and twenties business continued to grow and in late 1928 the company announced it had acquired property at the northwest corner of University Avenue and Queen Street (University had yet to be extended south of Queen to its present terminus at Front) on which another Canada Life Building would rise. On January 28 of the following year a sketch of the proposed new building prepared by the distinguished Canadian architectural firm of Sproatt and Rolph appeared in the local newspapers. However, for whatever reason (or reasons) the structure looked significantly different when it opened for business in mid-March 1931.

Above: The new Canada Life Building reamains as one of the most imposing structures on University Avenue. There was an attempt to have all new buildings on the avenue be just as imposing. That desire was never fulfilled.

Right: Workers put the finishing touches to the new beacon atop the Canada Life Building. Now a city landmark the beacon began providing weather prognostications on August 9, 1951. Note that the beacon encompasses the building's original flagpole.

Aside from the impressive appearance of the building its best-known feature is the 45-foot-high weather beacon that towers 321 feet above University Avenue. It consists of 1,007 bulbs in nineteen rows of lights and was first illuminated on August 9, 1951. The colour of the top beacon indicates the weather (Green = fair, Red = cloudy, Flashing Red = rain, Flashing White = snow) while the up and down direction of the lights forecasts the variation of the temperature (Up = warmer, Down = colder, Steady = no change). The forecasts (7:00 a.m. to midnight) are based on Environment Canada information and are updated four times a day.

September 13, 2009

The Day Noronic Went Up in Smoke

On September 20, 1949, pretty well all of Toronto's almost 700,000 citizens were in a state of shock following the recent burning of the Great Lakes passenger ship SS *Noronic* while berthed at the foot of Yonge Street. Toronto had been fortunate. A tragedy of a magnitude such as this one had never occurred in the city before. In fact, so unusual was such an event that even though the conflagration had taken place three days earlier the total number of victims was still undetermined. This in spite of the fact that one of the daily newspapers was reporting that 125 were dead, but, as one of its reporters warned, don't take that figure as the final count.

It took some time to conclude that the actual figure was 119: 118 passengers, all Americans, and one member of the crew, a Canadian who worked in the Purser's Office and died some weeks later from her injuries.

SS *Noronic* was launched at Port Arthur (now part of Thunder Bay) in 1913 and was described as "one of the finest examples of Canadian shipbuilding yet produced." Interestingly, in the newspaper story that described the interior of the new ship special emphasis was placed on "the beautiful mahogany and other fine woods" that adorned the vessel's dining and other public rooms. Little did anyone realize, as the years went by the enthusiastic care and upkeep of the wood trim through the use of dozens of coats of varnish and paint would contribute to the vessel's ultimate demise.

Noronic was not often seen here in Toronto, her usual ports of call being big cities on Lakes Erie, Michigan, and Superior. So it was that

SS *Noronic* was known as the "Queen of the Lakes" and was an infrequent visitor to the Port of Toronto. Her second trip to our city, where she arrived on September 16, 1949, would never be forgotten.

when she arrived early in the evening of September 16, 1949, many curious Torontonians wandered down to the waterfront to see the largest passenger ship on the Great Lakes known affectionately by many of her passengers as the "Queen of the Lakes."

Toronto was just one stop on the vessel's last trip of the 1949 season. The Welland Canal passage was spectacular. Then it was on to Hamilton,

The morning after, September 17, 1949, *Noronic* is a smouldering hulk as she lies in her berth near the foot of Yonge Street while the search for bodies continues.

followed by an overnight stay at the Canada Steamship Line's dock in Toronto. The next day the schedule called for a visit to Prescott and a tour through the Thousand Islands.

Unfortunately, a small fire that erupted in a linen closet early in the morning of September 17 quickly got out of control. The highly varnished and painted woodwork that had been admired at the vessel's launching fed the flames, and in short order that small fire had become an uncontrollable conflagration. *Noronic* was doomed.

Visitors to Mount Pleasant Cemetery can pay their respects to those victims of Toronto's worst disaster at the SS *Noronic* memorial in adjacent to the tree-lined avenue in Section 29.

September 20, 2009

The Word on the Street Is …

One of the most interesting features exhibited by virtually every small town or big city is the origin of many of their street names. Note that I said "many" names have interesting origins, since some were selected either because the word sounded nice (a fact that no doubt helps to sell houses situated on it) or because the term simply conjured up a pretty picture.

Here in Toronto there are more than 10,000 different streets and of those many fall into this latter category. Then there are those that remind us of some aspect of our city's history, be it an event (Pretoria Avenue, a battle during the South African War in which Canadians participated), a person (Yonge Street for Sir George Yonge, the Secretary of War in King George III's cabinet and a colleague of John Graves Simcoe) or a location (York Mills Road, or the mills on the Don River north of the Town of York).

While there are hundreds of other city streets that have fascinating name origins there are more than a few that baffle me. Take for instance the present Warden Avenue in Scarborough. Was it initially named because it was the road that led to the Path Warden, an important official who was responsible for the condition of the dusty thoroughfares in the rural townships that once surrounded the city? Seems like a logical answer, but what confuses me is an advertisement I found in an October 1913 edition of one of the city newspapers. The ad was promoting a planned real estate development at the quiet corner of Danforth and Wardin Avenues. Note the spelling of the latter street, which prompts the question: "Is that the

Warden AV
South | North

A typical Warden Avenue sign.

correct spelling and did someone alter the spelling to give us Warden?" If that's the case now all we need to do is find out who or what that word Wardin was all about.

Here's another strange one. The name of Pharmacy Avenue is so specific that there has to be a connection with a drug store. Or so one would believe. One evening while I was addressing a service club out in West Hill I asked if anyone knew the origins of any of Scarborough's old street names, especially Pharmacy. Suddenly an elderly lady in the audience piped up that when she lived on a farm not far from that street and any member of the family got sick and needed the family doctor's prescription filled it would be taken to the nearest drug store which was located at what is now the corner of St. Clair Avenue East and, wait for it, Pharmacy.

I'm hoping that someone at the Ontario College of Pharmacy can give me details about that old store since it would have been registered and is hopefully in the College archives. If and when I get those details I'll post them in a future column.

Having been unable to explain conclusively the origins of two prominent Scarborough street names here's one I can. Bellamy Road takes its name from American author Edward Bellamy, who wrote one of the nineteenth century's most popular books. Titled *Looking*

Author Edward Bellamy, who is honoured in the name of a Scarborough thoroughfare.

Backward 2000–1887, the book described a fictional utopian society that many of the book's readers were eager to establish for themselves. One such group sought to have Scarborough Township officials grant it a parcel of land on which the members would create a purely utopian lifestyle. While the township ultimately refused the request Bellamy's name soon connected with the dusty thoroughfare on which the proposed community was to be created.

September 27, 2009

Island Tunnel that Would Never Be

Over the years the most frequently heard expression, second only perhaps to the plaintive "wait 'til next year" cry offered up annually by Leaf/Argo/Blue Jay/Raptors fans, is "let's build a tunnel/bridge to the Island."

More recently yet another proposal for an Island connection was put forward, this time by the Toronto Port Authority. It was hoped that the $38 million cost would be covered in part with funds obtained from the federal government's infrastructure budget. Like every other project that attempted to connect the city with its Island, a treasure given to Toronto by Queen Victoria, the project died on the drawing board.

Historically, the Port Authority's plan was just another in a long list of similar projects all of which went nowhere.

In the late 1800s the privately owned public transportation company suggested connecting the city with the Island using a streetcar-only bridge. It would provide a way of getting financially challenged citizens to this marvellous summer playground across the bay using only a single fare and not the two required to take the streetcar to the ferry docks and another ticket to get on board the Island-bound ferry.

While nothing came of this or several other similar proposals it really looked as if an idea put forward in early 1935 might just come to fruition. As it would turn out it would be the only idea to even come close to happening. This plan would see the city connected by a vehicle

Construction of the new vehicle and pedestrian tunnel under the Western Channel got underway on October 7, 1935. It was to serve an airport that was still four years in the future. Construction was suddenly terminated just twenty-three days later. Note Maple Leaf Stadium at the southwest corner of Bathurst and Fleet (now Lake Shore Boulevard) in the left background.

The tunnel to Toronto Island proposal of 1935 was just one of many ideas suggested over the years. The pedestrian only structure seen in this sketch was proposed in 1959 by the TTC's new chairman Charles Walton who suggested it could be built for a mere $421,000.

and pedestrian tunnel with the west end of the Island. The impetus for building the $976,264 project was a proposal put forward by the Toronto Harbour Commissioners on June 7, 1935, to build the city's much-needed international airport on "the sandbar," a yet-to-be reclaimed area of Toronto Island that we now know as Hanlan's Point.

It was hoped that the scheme would be financed in great measure by the Dominion government as it struggled to get the nation out from under the effects of a major world depression.

Construction of the tunnel actually started on October 7, 1935, following approval of funding by the nation's Conservative government under R.B. Bennett. However, just one week later a national election was called and the Liberals under Mackenzie King won. The new prime minister quickly cancelled the city's tunnel project for reasons that some say had a lot to do with Sam McBride, a city alderman, an Island resident and, most importantly, a close friend of Mackenzie King. It also seems that Mackenzie King was not a big fan of the City of Toronto. No money, no tunnel.

Someone once said, the more things change, the more they stay the same.

October 11, 2009

A Revolutionary Condo Concept

There have been a variety of stories in the media about the proposed forty-two-storey condominium tower planned for the site of University Avenue's iconic Royal Canadian Military Institute. For obvious reasons

The Royal Canadian Military Institute is located on the west side of University Avenue just south of Dundas Street West. Note in this undated photo from the City of Toronto Archives there was a Graham-Paige car dealership next door to the north identified as Automobile and Supply Ltd. As this make was manufactured under this specific name only from 1928 until 1930 it's obvious that the photo was taken during this period.

Artist's sketch of the old building's façade as it is to be incorporated in the proposed new condominium. Note that a fire hydrant appears in the same location in both photos.

those stories placed emphasis on the new building and, in particular, the fact that almost all of its three-hundred-plus units will be sold without permanent parking spaces for vehicles. This is a revolutionary change in normal condo marketing techniques with emphasis placed on providing several hundred spaces for those who wish to get from here to there and back on, wait for it, a bicycle. Or by simply using the various streetcar, bus, and subway connections literally steps from the condo's front door.

What's been missing in these stories, and again for obvious reasons, is the history of the organization known as the Royal Canadian Military Institute and the old building that has stood for so long on University, which without some major work probably won't be standing for much longer.

Historically, today's RCMI has its origins in a meeting convened in early 1890 by Lieutenant-Colonel William Otter, a high-ranking officer in the Canadian Army. With the rapidly changing techniques of warfare, Otter's intention was to establish an association that would serve as a body for "the promotion and fostering of military art, science and literature in Canada." He used as examples similar organizations already flourishing in England, Australia, and the United States.

Following the meeting things were set in motion to formally establish what we know today as the Royal Canadian Military Institute. The first few meetings were held in rented rooms on King Street West and later in a three-storey house on what was then called Queen Street Avenue: a narrow thoroughfare later incorporated into today's much wider University Avenue.

It wasn't until 1906 that the Canadian Military Institute (the term Royal would be added much later) moved to its present site although the old house it initially occupied faced onto Simcoe Street, the side street one west of University. Over the next few years this house was remodeled and enlarged, a sort of "extreme makeover" that resulted in the club obtaining a University Avenue address. Though then listed at #96, the extension of University south of Queen in the late 1920s-early 1930s saw the entire street renumbered and today the RCMI is at 426 University Avenue.

October 18, 2009

Home Sweet Home Aboard Red Rocket

I have a question for you. When is a streetcar not just a streetcar? The answer, when it's turned into a residence. And for nearly one hundred old Toronto streetcars and trailers that's exactly what happened on October 4, 1922.

It was on this day that several communities, as well as a large number of outlying farms scattered over a 650 square mile swath of south Temiskaming in northern Ontario, were destroyed when forest fires ravaged the area. One of the hardest-hit towns was Haileybury, a community that had originally been settled in 1889 and named after the school in England that its founder Charles Farr had attended as a youngster.

The fire was fierce, and in less than six hours eleven citizens had been killed and 90 percent of the town's buildings wiped out. Suddenly more than 3,500 of the townsfolk found themselves homeless ... and winter was approaching.

Municipal and provincial officials were in a quandary. While food and other supplies were quick to arrive (as it had with the Halifax explosion five years before, the T. Eaton Company sent trainloads of necessities from its Toronto warehouses), the next biggest problem was finding some way to house the citizens. Forecasters were predicting snow within a few days.

Then came a surprising offer from Toronto's one-year-old municipally controlled public transit company, the Toronto Transportation

Courtesy of the Haileybury Heritage Museum.

Thanks to the TTC this former Toronto streetcar became "home sweet home" following the Haileybury fire in October 1922.

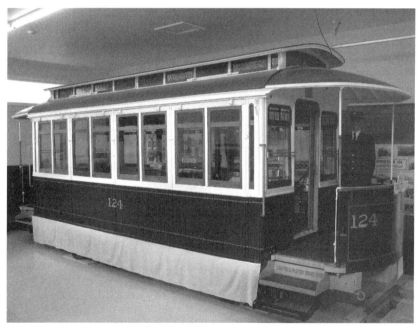

Courtesy of the Haileybury Heritage Museum.

One of the numerous old Toronto streetcars and trailers that provided shelter for the citizens of Haileybury.

Commission. It had acquired hundreds of old streetcars and trailers when it took over operations from the privately owned Toronto Railway Company (TRC) on September 1, 1921. These vehicles could easily serve as temporary houses. However, there were still ongoing discussions about the dollar value of these now obsolete pieces of equipment. And there were questions about how shipping some of them north to Haileybury would affect the final price that the city would have to pay for the purchase of the private company.

Nevertheless it was quickly decided that with winter approaching the need for housing was paramount, and it wasn't long before a total of 87 streetcars and trailers were on their way to not just Haileybury but to several other nearby communities that had also been affected by one of the worst forest fires in Canadian history.

Thanks to John Bromley for many of the details used in this story.

October 25, 2009

Let's Set the Record Straight

Before I begin this column, it's only proper that I preface it with a disclaimer. I have not yet watched the motion picture *Amelia*, a film that describes the life and times of the American-born aviatrix Amelia Earhart, but rumour has it that the movie is lacking in any significant reference to Miss Earhart's time here in Toronto. So I am here to set the record straight. It was during a speech given before the Canadian Club in December of 1932, a visit that took place just seven months after her record-setting solo flight across the Atlantic, that Miss Earhart announced to the audience that she had been "bitten by the aviation bug" while living in Toronto. That proclamation was confirmed by a similar statement made in Amelia's 1932 autobiography, *The Fun of It*.

The question is why was the twenty-year-old in Toronto in the first place? In her speech Amelia recounted that in 1917 she had come to Toronto from her home in Philadelphia to visit her sister who was attending St. Margaret's College on Bloor Street East. While here Amelia was appalled at the number of wounded and maimed young aviators returning from the front. She decided to stay and help as best she could. Joining the local VAD (Volunteer Aid Detachment) she became a nurse aide at the Spadina Military Hospital. As such she often visited the city's Royal Flying Corps airfields out in suburban Leaside and Armour Heights. And it was while watching aerial demonstrations at these two grass fields that Amelia Earhart was bitten by the "aviation bug."

The rest, as they say, is history.

Left: Amelia Earhart often remarked that she got the "flying bug" while serving as a nursing aide at Toronto's Spadina Military Hospital.

The Spadina Military Hospital was located in the former Knox Theological College that still stands on Spadina just north of College Street.

A rare photo of the Armour Heights airfield where Amelia caught "the aviation bug." Oh, and just because stunt flying was frowned upon doesn't mean it didn't happen.

November 1, 2009

Let's Head Back in Time

One of the few reminders we have of an earlier Toronto is the sound that emanates from the tower of Old City Hall whenever its trio of bells (the largest weighs 11,984 pounds, the next largest 2,915 pounds, and the smallest 1,907 pounds) ring out the time of day. The bells rang out for the first time just before midnight on December 31, 1900, in time to welcome the twentieth century. By then the city's new municipal building was more than a year old, having opened for business on September 18, 1899.

While it may seem strange that Toronto's new City Hall would be allowed to open to the public even though the hoisting of the bells and installation of the clock and intricate mechanism had yet to be done, it was done after a direct order was issued by the mayor of the day, John Shaw.

After many years of construction delays and enormous cost overruns, Shaw, as well as many members of his council, had become totally exasperated with a project that had first been proposed in 1887 at a cost of $300,000. Twelve years later the building still wasn't complete. By the time all the figures were in, the cost of Toronto's new City Hall would soar to nearly $2.5 million.

While the politicians argued over why the place took so long to build and why the costs had risen so dramatically, there was a very simple reason why the clock and bells were not in place in time for the opening ceremonies. For whatever reason, a letter confirming the

Toronto's third City Hall opened for business on September 18, 1899, even though the clock and trio of bells had yet to be installed in the tower. In this view we see the clock mechanism and in the background one of the huge clock faces.

purchase of the clock as well as its companion trio of bells at a total cost of $19,750 wasn't received by the manufacturer, Gillett and Johnston in Croydon, England, until just days before the scheduled opening of Toronto's new city hall on September 18, 1899.

It then took a little over a year for the bells to be cast. The complete order was then readied for shipment arriving in Toronto in mid-November, 1900. Finally on November 24 and 26, with a huge crowd in attendance both days, the bells were hoisted up the outside of the tower and deftly swung into place some 216 feet above Queen Street.

The clock mechanism, including the four 20-foot diameter glazed dial faces (among the largest in the world), followed.

As mentioned, the bells chimed for the first time to greet the twentieth century (January 1, 1901) although with the installation of the clock not yet complete, the actual ringing of the bells was done manually using pulleys and ropes. The clock itself wasn't set in motion until precisely noon on May 30, 1901, when Mayor Oliver Howland, using a pair of scissors, cut a ribbon that set the new clock's 500 pound pendulum in motion.

*   *   *

While on the subject of Toronto's beautiful Old City Hall, this structure was actually the third to hold that prestigious title. The first was located

Members of city hall staff inspect the newly arrived trio of bells destined for the clock tower of Toronto's newly constructed city hall, November 1900.

at the southwest corner of King and Jarvis Streets in the former town hall–market place combination that had served the citizens of York since being built in 1831.

In 1845 the city fathers and their appointed officials moved into a brand new building just down the street at the southwest corner of the Front and Jarvis intersection. A portion of this building, which served until architect Edward James Lennox's masterpiece at the top of Bay

Street, was ready in the fall of 1899 and still stands today, wrapped within the South St. Lawrence Market. The Council Chamber of this city hall, which was the second with that name but the first to be erected as an actual city hall, now serves as the Market Gallery where visitors are treated to fascinating exhibitions that portray the ever-changing face of our city.

And to complete the list, Toronto's present City Hall, the fourth with that title, was officially opened on September 13, 1965.

November 8, 2009

You Better Watch Out,
You Better Not Cry …

There are several traditions we celebrate here in our city without which, in my opinion, Toronto would be much the poorer. Going to the Island on the little ferryboats is a good example as is exploring the city through the windows of a TTC streetcar or seeing police officers patrol on their beautiful horses. I also believe it would be much less interesting without the St. Lawrence Hall, the Gooderham (Flatiron) Building, and Old City Hall (and, yes, even the New City Hall).

And there's one other long-time tradition that very nearly came to an abrupt and unexpected end. Not just Torontonians, but Canadians from coast to coast were stunned when officials of the iconic T. Eaton Co. announced on August 11, 1982, that effective immediately all work on preparing floats and costumes for that year's Santa Claus Parade would cease. It had been decided that for financial reasons Eaton's would no longer be prepared to sponsor an event that had become an integral part of the holiday season in Toronto ever since the very first Santa Claus Parade took to the city streets on a cold Saturday afternoon, December 2, 1905.

Actually, to call that day's event a parade is overstating what actually took place. The so-called parade, the brainchild of Timothy Eaton's twenty-nine-year-old son, John (later Sir John) Craig Eaton, consisted of nothing more than a few costumed Eaton employees who accompanied a horse-drawn wagon, on top of which was a somewhat bedraggled Santa

This newspaper ad for the 1918 Toronto Santa Claus Parade describes the route with the starting point at Yonge and Eglinton.

look-alike who tossed candy canes to the bemused crowd. The tiny group made its way from Toronto's old Union Station (several hundred yards west of the present station) and the Eaton department store near the Yonge and Queen intersection. Along the way the parade participants made sure the audience knew that there were great Christmas buys available at the Eaton store.

Over the years what started out as a small parade consisting of one horse-drawn wagon and a handful of marchers grew in size so that by 1981 the seventy-seventh edition of the annual event (the event had moved to Sundays in 1975) there were nearly thirty floats and 1,700 parade participants. However, no one knew it, but this parade would be memorable for another reason. It would be the last to be sponsored by Eaton's.

But many felt that this Toronto tradition was just too important to simply let fade way. Following the announcement made just a few months before the 1982 edition of the Eaton's Santa Claus Parade

A young and slightly bewildered Mike Filey meets Santa Claus in Eaton's Toyland following the 1944 edition of Eaton's Santa Claus Parade.

would step off for the seventy-eighth time, word of the cancellation was made public. Quickly, and under the guidance of Metro Toronto Chairman Paul Godfrey and local businessmen George Cohon and Ron Barbaro, a committee was formed, and within a few weeks twenty sponsors had committed enough money to resurrect the parade. What would be known as the Metro Santa Claus Parade returned to the streets of Toronto on November 14, 1982. The name has been modified, and today it's known as "The Santa Claus Parade."

And Santa, despite what my wife might tell you, I have been a good boy this year.

November 15, 2009

Flying Saucer of the Great White North

This past Remembrance Day, instead of attending the traditional services at Old City Hall (something that has occurred every November 11 since 1919), I decided to attend the service being held at the Canadian Air and Space Museum at Downsview Park. Attending were a few museum volunteers, some staff members, and a couple of dozen students from a nearby school. During the service I couldn't help looking over at the museum's full-size replica of the revolutionary Arrow jet interceptor that had been created from original plans and drawings by museum volunteers.

For those not old enough to remember, the original Arrow (that first flew in 1957) along with others that were to follow it off the assembly line were to protect us and our neighbors to the south from nuclear annihilation at the hands of those darn Russians whose bombers were waiting on the other side of the Arctic Circle.

As it turned out the Russians thought better of attacking us, which is just as well since the Diefenbaker government had already decided to cancel the contract that would have resulted in dozens of Arrows being built at Avro Canada's sprawling factory adjacent to Toronto's Malton (now Toronto Pearson International) Airport.

This wasn't the first time the government up in Ottawa put an end to a project that many experts believed would bring fame and glory to Canada's fledgling aviation history. Just eight years before the first Arrow

Avro Canada's C-102 Jetliner was North America's first jet-powered passenger aircraft. It first flew in the summer of 1949 and made its last flight on November 23, 1956.

flew, the same company startled the world when its C-102 Jetliner became North America's first jet-powered passenger transport and save for two weeks the world's first. That record is held by Great Britain's de Havilland Comet, several of which were to suffer catastrophic crashes.

Over the next few years the Jetliner was put through its paces, and soon officials of several airlines were considering adding the Canadian designed and built aircraft to their fleets. But it was not to be. The outbreak of war on the Korean peninsula in 1950 prompted the Canadian government to order Avro Canada to cease all work on the Jetliner and concentrate instead on the manufacture of the other aircraft on its assembly lines, the CF-100 jet interceptor. The possibility of the so-called Korean War escalating into a world war would soon end any chance that the Jetliner might have had to prove itself as a passenger aircraft. For the next few years the Jetliner carried out a number of utilitarian uses, with its last flight occurring on November 23, 1956. Shortly thereafter, and just as the completed and airworthy Arrows would be three years later, the Jetliner was cut into pieces. Another Canadian aviation dream died.

Any reference to Avro Canada's ill-fated Arrow and Jetliner would be incomplete without a brief mention of the company's flying saucer. This experimental aircraft, officially known as VZ-9AV and dubbed the Avrocar, was created during the mid 1950s–early 1960s to test the theory of combining vertical take-off and landing capabilities with

While the Canadian-designed and built Avrocar sure looked like a flying saucer, real flying was the last thing it could do.

high-performance characteristics. Though unsuccessful in both areas the Avrocar came at a time when Canada and Canadian companies were eager participants in the world of aviation.

To learn more about Canada's aviation history visit the Canadian Air and Space Museum at Downsview Park (*casmuseum.org*) or read any of Larry Milberry's fascinating books (*canavbooks.com*).

November 22, 2009

Shedding Light on Queen's Wharf Lighthouse

Over the past several decades the look of my city has changed dramatically, and not always for the better. While a few historic gems have been saved from the wreckers many more have vanished forever. Thanks for foresight of some anonymous Torontonians of eighty years ago, the tiniest of those gems can still be found in amongst the condo towers along the city's waterfront.

While the condo craze continues to sweep the Greater Toronto Area, who would have guessed that when the city's first condominiums (some of which began as "co-operatives") began appearing in Rosedale and on Avenue Road just north of St. Clair in the late 1960s they would be the precursors to this popular way of living?

Now found all over town, one area of the city where condo towers are particularly evident is the stretch of waterfront between Bathurst Street on the west to Parliament Street to the east.

In amongst the new condominiums and squeezed between the Lake Shore Boulevard and Fleet Street west of the Bathurst Street corner is a gem of a structure that reminds Torontonians of a time when the waters of the lake lapped at a city shoreline that was much further inland than the one we have today.

Erected in 1861 this lighthouse replaced an earlier, smaller structure that twenty-three years earlier had been placed on what was originally called the New Pier, a wooden jetty that jutted out into the Western

A crew moves the "ancient" Queen's Wharf lighthouse from where it originally stood near the Bathurst and Lake Shore Boulevard intersection to its present location several hundred feet further west. Note the two horses that dragged the structure over wooden rollers. The long-gone Maple Leaf Stadium is in the background. December 1929.

A pair of horses returns to the lighthouse. This time PC's Leisha Robinson on "Blue Moon" and Mike Dukasin on "Vimy Ridge" meet the TTC's historic PCC streetcar #4500 in front of the lighthouse exactly eighty years after the historic structure was moved. Thanks to Toronto Police Services Staff Inspector William Wardle for arranging this photo opportunity.

Channel just north of the present Bathurst and Lake Shore Boulevard intersection. For many years these signals were instrumental in guiding all forms of sailing vessels attempting to enter an often dangerous passageway into Toronto Harbour.

When harbour officials determined that the Western Channel had become too dangerous and that no warning signals of any type could prevent accidents it was decided to build a new, deeper channel further to the south. When this work was completed around 1912, the lighthouse, now referred to as the Queen's Wharf lighthouse following the pier's renaming to honour the immensely popular Queen Victoria, was left high and dry.

It stood far from the new channel for many years until some anonymous soul decided the structure was actually worth preserving. In early December of 1929 the lighthouse was lifted onto a series of wooden rollers and pulled by a pair of horses to a small parcel of land west of its original site where it stood right on the water's edge. This new location far from the water helps give citizens some idea on just how much land filling has taken place over the years.

November 29, 2009

Toronto's Ever-Changing Skyline

L ast week I wrote about the tiny Queen's Wharf lighthouse that sits on
the north side of Lake Shore Boulevard just west of the busy Bathurst

Toronto's skyline in 1949. The pioneer skyscrapers (left to right) include Canada Life
(without the weather beacon), the Royal York Hotel (for a time the largest hotel in the
country), the new Bank of Nova Scotia (its construction interrupted by the Second
World War), and the Bank of Commerce (at the time the tallest building in the entire
British Commonwealth — remember that term?).

Photo by John McQuarrie.

Toronto's skyline exactly sixty years later — far too many buildings to try and identify.

Street intersection. Originally a lonely sentinel guiding ships into Toronto Harbour through the old Western Channel (it was filled in and the site is now occupied by the Lake Shore-Bathurst intersection), the lighthouse was moved in 1929 to its present location where several modern new condominiums tower over it.

While that part of the city's western waterfront has seen great changes, so too has the central waterfront as the photos that accompany this column will testify. The 1949 view is cluttered with non-descript storage warehouses and at the extreme left, the TTC-operated Toronto Island ferry service with the recently restored *Trillium* in its own slip. Launched in 1910 *Trillium* will reach the century mark on June 18, 2010.

To the extreme right is the popular *Cayuga*, which operated between Toronto and a trio of Niagara River ports, Niagara-on-the-Lake, Queenston, and Lewiston for nearly a half-century. It's obvious from the photo that another prime use of the waterfront was as a place to park cars. While there were pay lots many of the drivers took advantage of a time before parking meters.

In addition, the impact the cross-waterfront railway viaduct had on the construction of any structures close to water's edge is apparent in this view. Only the Toronto Harbour Commission Building, which was erected in 1918–19 right on the water's edge, and the nearby Postal Delivery

235

Building (now the site of the Air Canada Centre) appear to have intruded on this "no man's land." Incidentally, visible in this view is the gleaming white south façade of the Postal Delivery Building that incorporates a portion of the building's original bas-relief mural that depicts the history of communications and transportation.

As the second photo shows sixty years have passed and now condos, hotels and office buildings have made their way right down to the edge of the Bay.

December 6, 2009

The Rise of the Big Smoke

As we approach the end of 2009, a year that marks 175 years of Toronto's incorporation as a city, it's interesting to examine how our city has grown from a tiny community nestled in a forest clearing on the edge of a pristine bay to the sprawling metropolis the world knows and respects today.

The year was 1793 when John Graves Simcoe, the lieutenant governor of the newly established Province of Upper Canada, selected a site on the shoreline of pristine Lake Ontario (a site that was well protected by a long curving peninsula that years later would become Toronto Island) as the location of a shipyard. It was here, at a place Simcoe named York (after King George III's second eldest son, Frederick, the Duke of York) that naval vessels would be constructed to help protect against imminent invasion by forces of the new republic south of the border. The hostilities that the governor had predicted finally erupted in 1812. Known by many back then as "President Madison's War" we recognize that conflict today as the "War of 1812."

Following the signing of the Treaty of Ghent (a city then in the Netherlands, now in Belgium) on Christmas Eve, 1814, peace soon returned and it wasn't long before Simcoe's little town began to prosper. However, York's minor political status as a town continued to hinder the growing community's progress. Eventually, provincial authorities agreed to elevate the Town of York to city status. Effective March 6, 1834, the new City of Toronto (its original name having been reinstated) and its 9,254 citizens could now look to the future.

Looking north on a dusty Yonge Street from just north of Eglinton Avenue in the old Town of North Toronto, circa 1903. Approaching the photographer is one of the heavy electric streetcars operated by the privately owned Toronto and York Radial Railway. It was in 1909 that Torontonians began riding these cars all the way to Sutton near Lake Simcoe.

Courtesy of CS&P Architects.

This sketch shows The Republic, a new Tridel condominium under construction at 25 Broadway Avenue. The nearby North Toronto Collegiate Institute will be demolished and a new NTCI will occupy the low-rise building located between the two condo towers.

One of the most powerful tools awarded to the city by the province was the authority to tax personal real estate thereby giving Toronto a way to raise money to build and maintain such "infrastructure" items as sidewalks, sewers, and eventually water mains. Sound familiar?

As the years went by, Toronto grew and became more prosperous. Before long several "satellite" communities began to spring up just outside the city's original boundaries (which were, roughly, the modern Bloor Street, Dufferin Street, and the Don River to the north, west, and east, respectively). Outside the city, taxes were non-existent so living appeared to be cheaper.

However, just as had befallen the old Town of York years earlier, the dramatic growth of these outlying towns and villages soon necessitated a supply of clean water, proper sewers, and waste treatment facilities, road and sidewalk improvements, and the like. With the inability to tax their own citizens to fund these items and the obvious reluctance of the province to create more cities with taxing powers, it soon became evident that a takeover by the big city of Toronto was the only answer.

The first of these takeovers (actually the term "annexation" was used no doubt because it sounded less big brother-like, even though it was) was the Town of Yorkville, nestled on the northern fringes of the city. That annexation took place in 1883 and it was followed the next year by Brockton on the city's western boundary and Riverdale (known for a time as Riverside) just across the Don River.

The annexations continued until a total of thirty-two individual communities as well as parcels of land and water lots (included in the latter were the Helliwell Farm in 1912 and part of Humber Bay nine years before) had come into the fold. An interesting piece of Toronto trivia is the fact that what is known today as The Annex was a name given to the history-rich neighbourhood created by two separate annexations, the first in 1887 and the second in 1906.

The last major land annexation occurred on December 15, 1912, when the four square miles known as the Town of North Toronto plus its 6,655 citizens became part of Toronto.

Just eight days before the annexation took place the cornerstone of the town's new high school was tapped into place. North Toronto Collegiate Institute would grow to become one of the nation's finest high schools.

December 13, 2009

Rolling Billboards of the Past

As controversial as the recent attempt to promote doing "you know what" through the use of advertising "wraps" on a few TTC streetcars

Photo by John Bromley.

During the Great War the TTC's predecessor, the Toronto Railway Company, used a few of their streetcars as moving billboards to entice recruits to join up. Here work car #6 promotes the #1 Construction (Overseas) Battalion.

The busy Queen and Bay intersection in the summer of 1941. Note the fellows in uniform, the ACE theatre and its marquee and the small Dominion store, a forerunner to the rambling supermarkets that now go under the name Metro. The latter two structures stand close to the site of today's Simpson's Tower.

turned out to be, the actual concept of promoting goods and services on the outside and/or inside of TTC vehicles is not a new idea. Thanks to information gleaned from Ted Wickson, who spent many years in the Commission's Advertising Department before becoming responsible for the TTC's archives, the use of transit vehicles as a means to promote ideas or products is certainly not a new technique.

In fact, as far back as the First World War the TTC's predecessor, the Toronto Railway Company, had several of their streetcars decorated with banners and large signs enticing young Torontonians to join one of the several military units being formed in Toronto. To do this, these decorated "patriotic vehicles" would wander the main downtown streets with senior members of the various regiments appealing to young men in the crowd to climb aboard and sign up. Often there'd be a military band nearby playing patriotic airs to stir emotions.

With the return of peace, vehicular traffic increased on the city streets. So too did the number of accidents with "flivvers" either bouncing off streetcars or knocking down pedestrians. This resulted in the Ontario Safety League placing what were called "car cards" in special holders on the on the exterior of the TTC vehicles. These notices encouraged caution when approaching a streetcar and reminding drivers to stop behind the vehicle's open doors, a rule that's still in effect.

Soon ads for popular consumer products of the era such as OXO and Turret cigarettes were bringing in much-needed revenue. Before long, a wide variety of advertising cards found their way inside the Commission's streetcars and the recently introduced gasoline buses. In the Queen and Bay photo accompanying this column note the ad for Joy gasoline on the front of the PCC streetcar.

With the opening of the new Yonge subway in 1954 advertising cards made their way inside the shiny new red Gloucester cars as well. Gave people something to do and read if staring at your fellow passengers was not your style.

At about this same time the TTC decorated several of its buses with painted wreathes and ribbons and messages that announced "Merry Christmas," a simple greeting that would no doubt be unacceptable today.

The biggest change in the method of advertising on transit vehicles came in 1984 when five of the Commission's streetcars were given a total hand-painted treatment ("total wraps" to use the industry's term) to honour the city's 150th anniversary and the province's 200th.

These were followed two years later by the first "total paint" bus when one of the GM "fishbowls" became the "Milk Bus" sporting a hand painted wrap paid for by the Ontario Milk Producers.

By the early 1990s the advertising industry had perfected a method of printing colourful messages on supersize pieces of vinyl that could then be easily wrapped around and removed from (after a contracted length of time) TTC streetcars and buses while all the while ensuring that exacting TTC safety standards were maintained.

It's a long way from the jingoistic streetcars of 1914–18 to the sometimes controversial and occasionally overwhelming "wrapped" transit vehicles of today.

December 20, 2009

They Were a Cut Above

In last week's column I took a look back on the various types of advertising that has appeared on Toronto public transit vehicles over the years. While there has never been a problem promoting brands of gasoline (such as Joy,

Queen Street looking west towards the Victoria Street intersection in December 1954. Note the sign for the Town Tavern that was located at 16 Queen Street East and was one of the city's favourite night clubs for many years. The Filey family would occasionally visit the nearby Town Bar-B-Q for one of its scrumptious chicken or beef torpedoes.

NEW YEAR'S EVE FROLIC

C.N.E. AUTOMOTIVE BUILDING

Featuring **"THE CREW CUTS"**

with **ELLIS McLINTOCK**

$5.00 PER COUPLE

DUE TO THE OUT-OF-TOWN DEMAND
TICKETS ON SALE AT THE DOOR
ALSO AT MOODEY'S AND MEYERS TICKET AGENCIES OR PHONE ME. 4697
MANY VALUABLE PRIZES—TRIPS TO NEW YORK, ETC.

A BULOVA WATCH FREE!
EVERY 30 MINUTES FROM
9 P.M. UNTIL 3 A.M.
COURTESY OF MORSE CREDIT JEWELLERS

A newspaper ad promoting the appearance of Toronto's own pop music sensations, the Crew Cuts at the CNE's Automotive Building on New Year's Eve, 1954.

Lion, or Cities Service) can you remember a time when, unlike today, it was also perfectly okay to feature ads on TTC streetcars and buses that promoted the use of such cigarette brands as Buckingham, Winchester, Turrets, and Sweet Caporal? And for years even liquor and beer ads were perfectly acceptable, with ads for O'Keefe, Brading's, and Old Vienna.

During the Second World War, ads seeking the public's attention to the purchase of Victory Bonds to help finance the war were frequently seen on TTC vehicles. With the return of peacetime ads began the promotion of all kinds of public shows and events being held around town. Some examples are the Home Show at the now demolished Mutual Arena on (where else?) Mutual Street in the heart of the city, the appearance of high-priced American talent featured each year at the CNE Grandstand, and the annual show of new cars and trucks inside the CNE's massive Automotive Building.

And while we're on the subject of the CNE's Automotive Building, which has recently been beautifully reborn as the Allstream Conference Centre, a close examination of the photo accompanying this column reveals another type of event that was held in the building.

New Year's Eve, 1954, was not far away when this eastbound Queen streetcar, seen in the accompanying photo, crossed the Victoria Street intersection. Close inspection of one of its advertising cards reveals that a special attraction at the Auto Building that New Year's Eve would be Toronto's pop singing group, the Crew Cuts. The boys were back in their hometown performing at the old Casino Theatre on Queen Street West after a very successful stint at various clubs south of the border. Admission to the New Year's Eve show was $5 per couple. And with the interest shown from out-of-towners a quantity of tickets was made available at the door to anyone who took the time to drive all the way to Toronto. Nice touch.

The group got its start in the early 1950s at St. Michael's Boys Choir School on Bond Street where the Four Lads, another famous Toronto singing group, had its beginnings. (A third successful pop group known as The Diamonds began its career singing in the basement of the Church of St. Thomas Aquinas in the Eglinton and Dufferin neighbourhood.) One of the Crew Cuts earliest boosters was Barry Nesbitt, who initially knew the group as the Canadaires and gave the boys their first radio exposure on his CKFH radio show. As time passed and the boys got more exposure their career began to blossom. It was following an appearance on an American radio show that the host, observing that all four boys sported similar haircuts, selected the name by the boys would become known.

Anyone that grew up in the mid-1950s will recognize the Crew Cuts most famous recording, "Sh-Boom," which made it to Number One on the North American Hit Parade in 1954.

December 27, 2009